Verbum Domini

The Word of God in the Life and Mission of the Church

POPE BENEDICT XVI

POST-SYNODAL
APOSTOLIC EXHORTATION
VERBUM DOMINI
OF THE HOLY FATHER
BENEDICT XVI
TO THE BISHOPS, CLERGY,
CONSECRATED PERSONS
AND THE LAY FAITHFUL
ON THE WORD OF GOD
IN THE LIFE AND MISSION
OF THE CHURCH

Copyright © 2010 by Libreria Editrice Vaticana
Vatican City

All rights reserved

Published by The Word Among Us Press
7115 Guilford Road
Frederick, Maryland 21704
www.wau.org

15 14 13 12 11   2 3 4 5 6

ISBN: 978-1-59325-193-2

Cover design by David Crosson
Cover photography Catholic News Service

No part of this publication may be reproduced, stored in a retrieval
system, or transmitted in any form or by any means—electronic,
mechanical, photocopy, recording, or any other—except for brief
quotations in printed reviews, without the prior permission of the
author and publisher.

Made and printed in the United States of America

INTRODUCTION

1. "THE WORD OF THE LORD abides for ever. This word is the Gospel which was preached to you" (*1 Pet* 1:25; cf. *Is* 40:8). With this assertion from the First Letter of Saint Peter, which takes up the words of the Prophet Isaiah, we find ourselves before the mystery of God, who has made himself known through the gift of his word. This word, which abides for ever, entered into time. God spoke his eternal Word humanly; his Word "became flesh" (*Jn* 1:14). This is the good news. This is the proclamation which has come down the centuries to us today. The Twelfth Ordinary General Assembly of the Synod of Bishops, meeting in the Vatican from 5-26 October 2008, had as its theme: *The Word of God in the Life and Mission of the Church*. It was a profound experience of encounter with Christ, the Word of the Father, who is present where two or three are gathered in his name (cf. *Mt* 18:20). With this Post-Synodal Apostolic Exhortation I readily respond to the request of the Synod Fathers to make known to the whole People of God the rich fruits which emerged from the synodal sessions and the recommendations which resulted from

our common endeavour.[1] Consequently, I intend to revisit the work of the Synod in the light of its documents: the *Lineamenta*, the *Instrumentum Laboris*, the *Relationes ante* and *post disceptationem*, the texts of the interventions, both those delivered on the Synod floor and those presented in written form, the reports of the smaller discussion groups, the Final Message to the People of God and, above all, a number of specific proposals (*Propositiones*) which the Fathers considered especially significant. In this way I wish to point out certain fundamental approaches to a rediscovery of God's word in the life of the Church as a wellspring of constant renewal. At the same time I express my hope that the word will be ever more fully at the heart of every ecclesial activity.

That our joy may be complete

2.   Before all else, I would like to call to mind the beauty and pleasure of the renewed encounter with the Lord Jesus which we experienced during the synodal assembly. In union with with the Synod Fathers, then, I address all the faithful in the words of Saint John in his first letter: "We proclaim to you the eternal life which was with the Father and which was made manifest to us – that which we have seen and heard we proclaim also to you, so that you may have fellowship with us; and our fellowship is with the Father and with his

---

[1] Cf. *Propositio* 1.

Son Jesus Christ" (*1 Jn* 1:2-3). The Apostle speaks to us of *hearing, seeing, touching and looking upon* (cf. *1 Jn* 1:1) the word of life, since life itself was made manifest in Christ. Called to communion with God and among ourselves, we must proclaim this gift. From this kerygmatic standpoint, the synodal assembly was a testimony, before the Church and before the world, to the immense beauty of encountering the word of God in the communion of the Church. For this reason I encourage all the faithful to renew their personal and communal encounter with Christ, the word of life made visible, and to become his heralds, so that the gift of divine life – communion – can spread ever more fully throughout the world. Indeed, sharing in the life of God, a Trinity of love, is *complete joy* (cf. *1 Jn* 1:4). And it is the Church's gift and unescapable duty to communicate that joy, born of an encounter with the person of Christ, the Word of God in our midst. In a world which often feels that God is superfluous or extraneous, we confess with Peter that he alone has "the words of eternal life" (*Jn* 6:68). There is no greater priority than this: to enable the people of our time once more to encounter God, the God who speaks to us and shares his love so that we might have life in abundance (cf. *Jn* 10:10).

From "Dei Verbum" to the Synod on the Word of God

3.   With the Twelfth Ordinary General Assembly of the Synod of Bishops on the Word of God,

we were conscious of dealing in a certain sense with the very *heart* of the Christian life, in continuity with the previous synodal assembly on *The Eucharist as the Source and Summit of the Church's Life and Mission*. Indeed, the Church is built upon the word of God; she is born from and lives by that word.[2] Throughout its history, the People of God has always found strength in the word of God, and today too the ecclesial community grows by hearing, celebrating and studying that word. It must be acknowledged that in recent decades ecclesial life has grown more sensitive to this theme, particularly with reference to Christian revelation, the living Tradition and sacred Scripture. Beginning with the pontificate of Pope Leo XIII, we can say that there has been a crescendo of interventions aimed at an increased awareness of the importance of the word of God and the study of the Bible in the life of the Church,[3] culminating in the Second Vatican Council and specifically in the promulgation of the Dogmatic Constitution on Divine Revelation *Dei Verbum*. The latter represented a milestone in the Church's history: "The Synod Fathers ... acknowledge with gratitude the great benefits which this document brought to the life of the Church, on the exegetical, theological,

---

[2] Cf. TWELFTH ORDINARY GENERAL ASSEMBLY OF THE SYNOD OF BISHOPS, *Instrumentum Laboris*, 27.

[3] Cf. LEO XIII, Encyclical Letter *Providentissimus Deus* (18 November 1893): ASS 26 (1893-94), 269-292; BENEDICT XV, Encyclical Letter *Spiritus Paraclitus* (15 September 1920): AAS 12 (1920), 385-422; PIUS XII, Encyclical Letter *Divino Afflante Spiritu* (30 September 1943): AAS 35 (1943), 297-325.

spiritual, pastoral and ecumenical plane".[4] The intervening years have also witnessed a growing awareness of the "trinitarian and salvation-historical horizon of revelation"[5] against which Jesus Christ is to be acknowledged as "mediator and fullness of all revelation".[6] To each generation the Church unceasingly proclaims that Christ "completed and perfected revelation. Everything to do with his presence and his self-manifestation was involved in achieving this: his words and works, signs and miracles, but above all his death and resurrection from the dead, and finally his sending of the Spirit of truth".[7]

Everyone is aware of the great impulse which the Dogmatic Constitution *Dei Verbum* gave to the revival of interest in the word of God in the life of the Church, to theological reflection on divine revelation and to the study of sacred Scripture. In the last forty years, the Church's magisterium has also issued numerous statements on these questions.[8] By celebrating this Synod, the

[4] *Propositio* 2.

[5] *Ibid.*

[6] SECOND VATICAN ECUMENICAL COUNCIL, Dogmatic Constitution on Divine Revelation *Dei Verbum*, 2.

[7] *Ibid.*, 4

[8] Noteworthy among various kinds of interventions are: PAUL VI, Apostolic Letter *Summi Dei Verbum* (4 November 1963): AAS 55 (1963), 979-995; Motu Proprio *Sedula Cura* (27 June 1971): AAS 63 (1971), 665-669; JOHN PAUL II, *General Audience* (1 May 1985): *L'Osservatore Romano*, 2-3 May 1985, p. 6; *Address on the Interpretation of the Bible in the Church* (23 April 1993): AAS 86 (1994), 232-243; BENEDICT XVI, *Address to the International Congress held on the Fortieth Anniversary of "Dei Verbum"* (16 September 2005): AAS 97 (2005), 957; *Angelus* (6 November

Church, conscious of her continuing journey under the guidance of the Holy Spirit, felt called to further reflection on the theme of God's word, in order to review the implementation of the Council's directives, and to confront the new challenges which the present time sets before Christian believers.

The Synod of Bishops on the Word of God

4. In the twelfth synodal assembly, Bishops from throughout the world gathered around the word of God and symbolically placed the text of the Bible at the centre of the assembly, in order to stress anew something we risk taking for granted in everyday life: *the fact that God speaks and responds to our questions.*[9] Together we listened to and celebrated the word of the Lord. We recounted to one another all that the Lord is doing in the midst of the People of God, and we shared our hopes and concerns. All this made us realize that we can deepen our relationship with the word of God

2005): *Insegnamenti* I (2005), 759-760. Also worthy of mention are the interventions of the PONTIFICAL BIBLICAL COMMISSION, *De Sacra Scriptura et Christologia* (1984): *Enchiridion Vaticanum* 9, Nos. 1208-1339; *Unity and Diversity in the Church* (11 April 1988): *Enchiridion Vaticanum* 11, Nos. 544-643; *The Interpretation of the Bible in the Church* (15 April 1993): *Enchiridion Vaticanum* 13, Nos. 2846-3150; *The Jewish People and their Sacred Scriptures in the Christian Bible* (24 May 2001): *Enchiridion Vaticanum* 20, Nos. 733-1150; *The Bible and Morality. Biblical Roots of Christian Conduct* (11 May 2008): Vatican City, 2008.

[9] Cf. BENEDICT XVI, *Address to the Roman Curia* (22 December 2008): AAS 101 (2009), 49.

only within the "we" of the Church, in mutual listening and acceptance. Hence our gratitude for the testimonies about the life of the Church in different parts of the world which emerged from the various interventions on the floor. It was also moving to hear the fraternal delegates, who accepted our invitation to take part in the synodal meeting. I think in particular of the meditation offered to us by His Holiness Bartholomaios I, Ecumenical Patriarch of Constantinople, for which the Fathers expressed deep appreciation.[10] Furthermore, for the first time ever, the Synod of Bishops also invited a rabbi to offer us a precious witness on the Hebrew Scriptures, which are also part of our own sacred Scriptures.[11]

In this way we were able to acknowledge with joy and gratitude that "in the Church there is also a Pentecost today – in other words, the Church speaks in many tongues, and not only outwardly, in the sense that all the great languages of the world are represented in her, but, more profoundly, inasmuch as present within her are various ways of experiencing God and the world, a wealth of cultures, and only in this way do we come to see the vastness of the human experience and, as a result, the vastness of the word of God".[12] We

[10] Cf. *Propositio* 37.

[11] Cf. PONTIFICAL BIBLICAL COMMISSION, *The Jewish People and their Sacred Scriptures in the Christian Bible* (24 May 2001): *Enchiridion Vaticanum* 20, Nos. 733-1150.

[12] BENEDICT XVI, *Address to the Roman Curia* (22 December 2008): AAS 101 (2009), 50.

were also able to see an ongoing Pentecost; various peoples are still waiting for the word of God to be proclaimed in their own language and in their own culture.

How can I fail to mention that throughout the Synod we were accompanied by the testimony of the Apostle Paul! It was providential that the Twelfth Ordinary General Assembly took place during the year dedicated to the great Apostle of the Nations on the two thousandth anniversary of his birth. Paul's life was completely marked by his zeal for the spread of God's word. How can we not be moved by his stirring words about his mission as a preacher of the word of God: "I do everything for the Gospel" (*1 Cor* 9:23); or, as he writes in the *Letter to the Romans*: "I am not ashamed of the Gospel; it is the power of God for salvation to every one who has faith" (1:16). Whenever we reflect on the word of God in the life and mission of the Church, we cannot but think of Saint Paul and his life spent in spreading the message of salvation in Christ to all peoples.

The Prologue of John's Gospel as a guide

5.   With this Apostolic Exhortation I would like the work of the Synod to have a real effect on the life of the Church: on our personal relationship with the sacred Scriptures, on their interpretation in the liturgy and catechesis, and in scientific research, so that the Bible may not be simply a word from the past, but a living and timely word. To ac-

complish this, I would like to present and develop the labours of the Synod by making constant reference to the *Prologue of John's Gospel* (*Jn* 1:1-18), which makes known to us the basis of our life: the Word, who from the beginning is with God, who became flesh and who made his dwelling among us (cf. *Jn* 1:14). This is a magnificent text, one which offers a synthesis of the entire Christian faith. From his personal experience of having met and followed Christ, John, whom tradition identifies as "the disciple whom Jesus loved" (*Jn* 13:23; 20:2; 21:7, 20), "came to a deep certainty: Jesus is the Wisdom of God incarnate, he is his eternal Word who became a mortal man".[13] May John, who "saw and believed" (cf. *Jn* 20:8) also help us to lean on the breast of Christ (cf. *Jn* 13:25), the source of the blood and water (cf. *Jn* 19:34) which are symbols of the Church's sacraments. Following the example of the Apostle John and the other inspired authors, may we allow ourselves to be led by the Holy Spirit to *an ever greater love of the word of God.*

[13] Cf. BENEDICT XVI, *Angelus* (4 January 2009): *Insegnamenti* V, 1 (2009), 13.

PART ONE

VERBUM DEI

*"In the beginning was the Word,
and the Word was with God,
and the Word was God…
and the Word became flesh"*
(Jn 1:1, 14)

THE GOD WHO SPEAKS

God in dialogue

6. The novelty of biblical revelation consists in the fact that God becomes known through the dialogue which he desires to have with us.[14] The Dogmatic Constitution *Dei Verbum* had expressed this by acknowledging that the unseen God "from the fullness of his love, addresses men and women as his friends, and lives among them, in order to invite and receive them into his own company".[15] Yet we would not yet sufficiently grasp the message of the Prologue of Saint John if we stopped at the fact that God enters into loving communion with us. In reality, the Word of God, through whom "all things were made" (*Jn* 1:3) and who "became flesh" (*Jn* 1:14), is the same Word who is "in the beginning" (*Jn* 1:1). If we realize that this is an allusion to the beginning of the book of Genesis (cf. *Gen* 1:1), we find ourselves faced with *a beginning* which is absolute and which speaks to us of the inner life of God. The Johannine Prologue makes us realize that the

[14] Cf. *Relatio ante disceptationem*, I.
[15] SECOND VATICAN ECUMENICAL COUNCIL, Dogmatic Constitution on Divine Revelation *Dei Verbum*, 2.

Logos is truly *eternal*, and from eternity *is himself God*. God was never without his *Logos*. The Word exists before creation. Consequently at the heart of the divine life there is communion, there is absolute gift. "God is love" (*1 Jn* 4:16), as the same Apostle tells us elsewhere, thus pointing to "the Christian image of God and the resulting image of mankind and its destiny".[16] God makes himself known to us as a mystery of infinite love in which the Father eternally utters his Word in the Holy Spirit. Consequently the Word, who from the beginning is with God and is God, reveals God himself in the dialogue of love between the divine persons, and invites us to share in that love. Created in the image and likeness of the God who is love, we can thus understand ourselves only in accepting the Word and in docility to the work of the Holy Spirit. In the light of the revelation made by God's Word, the enigma of the human condition is definitively clarified.

The analogy of the word of God

7.   In the light of these considerations, born of meditation on the Christian mystery expressed in the Prologue of John, we now need to consider what the Synod Fathers affirmed about the different ways in which we speak of "the word of God". They rightly referred to a symphony of

---

[16] BENEDICT XVI, Encyclical Letter *Deus Caritas Est* (25 December 2005), 1: AAS 98 (2006), 217-218.

the word, to a single word expressed in multiple ways: "a polyphonic hymn".[17] The Synod Fathers pointed out that human language operates analogically in speaking of the word of God. In effect, this expression, while referring to God's self-communication, also takes on a number of different meanings which need to be carefully considered and related among themselves, from the standpoint both of theological reflection and pastoral practice. As the Prologue of John clearly shows us, the *Logos* refers in the first place to the eternal Word, the only Son, begotten of the Father before all ages and consubstantial with him: *the word was with God, and the word was God.* But this same Word, Saint John tells us, "became flesh" (*Jn* 1:14); hence Jesus Christ, born of the Virgin Mary, is truly the Word of God who has become consubstantial with us. Thus the expression "word of God" here refers to the person of Jesus Christ, the eternal Son of the Father, made man.

While the Christ event is at the heart of divine revelation, we also need to realize that creation itself, the *liber naturae*, is an essential part of this symphony of many voices in which the one word is spoken. We also profess our faith that God has spoken his word in salvation history; he has made his voice heard; by the power of his Spirit "he has spoken through the prophets".[18] God's word is thus spoken throughout the history of salvation,

---

[17] *Instrumentum Laboris*, 9.
[18] *Nicene-Constantinopolitan Creed*: DS 150.

and most fully in the mystery of the incarnation, death and resurrection of the Son of God. Then too, the word of God is that word preached by the Apostles in obedience to the command of the Risen Jesus: "Go into all the world and preach the Gospel to the whole creation" (*Mk* 16:15). The word of God is thus handed on in the Church's living Tradition. Finally, the word of God, attested and divinely inspired, is sacred Scripture, the Old and New Testaments. All this helps us to see that, while in the Church we greatly venerate the sacred Scriptures, the Christian faith is not a "religion of the book": Christianity is the "religion of the word of God", not of "a written and mute word, but of the incarnate and living Word".[19] Consequently the Scripture is to be proclaimed, heard, read, received and experienced as the word of God, in the stream of the apostolic Tradition from which it is inseparable.[20]

As the Synod Fathers stated, the expression "word of God" is used analogically, and we should be aware of this. The faithful need to be better helped to grasp the different meanings of the expression, but also to understand its unitary sense. From the theological standpoint too, there is a need for further study of how the different meanings of this expression are interrelated, so that the unity of God's plan and, within it, the

---

[19] SAINT BERNARD OF CLAIRVAUX, *Homilia super missus est*, IV, 11: PL 183, 86B.
[20] Cf. SECOND VATICAN ECUMENICAL COUNCIL, Dogmatic Constitution on Divine Revelation *Dei Verbum*, 10.

centrality of the person of Christ, may shine forth more clearly.[21]

The cosmic dimension of the word

8.   When we consider the basic meaning of the word of God as a reference to the eternal Word of God made flesh, the one Saviour and mediator between God and humanity,[22] and we listen to this word, we are led by the biblical revelation to see that it is the foundation of all reality. The Prologue of Saint John says of the divine *Logos*, that "all things were made through him, and without him was not anything made that was made" (*Jn* 1:3); and in the *Letter to the Colossians* it is said of Christ, "the first-born of all creation" (1:15), that "all things were created through him and for him" (1:16). The author of the *Letter to the Hebrews* likewise states that "by faith we understand that the world was created by the word of God, so that what is seen was made out of things which do not appear" (11:3).

For us, this proclamation is a word of freedom. Scripture tells us that everything that exists does not exist by chance but is willed by God and part of his plan, at whose center is the invitation to partake, in Christ, in the divine life. Creation

---

[21]   Cf. *Propositio* 3.
[22]   Cf. CONGREGATION FOR THE DOCTRINE OF THE FAITH, Declaration on the Unicity and Salvific Universality of Jesus Christ and of the Church *Dominus Iesus* (6 August 2000), 13-15: AAS 92 (2000), 754-756.

is born of the *Logos* and indelibly bears the mark of the *creative Reason which orders and directs it*; with joy-filled certainty the psalms sing: "By the word of the Lord the heavens were made, and all their host by the breath of his mouth" (*Ps* 33:6); and again, "he spoke, and it came to be; he commanded, and it stood forth" (*Ps* 33:9). All reality expresses this mystery: "The heavens are telling the glory of God; and the firmament proclaims his handiwork" (*Ps* 19:1). Thus sacred Scripture itself invites us to acknowledge the Creator by contemplating his creation (cf. *Wis* 13:5; *Rom* 1:19-20). The tradition of Christian thought has developed this key element of the symphony of the word, as when, for example, Saint Bonaventure, who in the great tradition of the Greek Fathers sees all the possibilities of creation present in the *Logos*,[23] states that "every creature is a word of God, since it proclaims God".[24] The Dogmatic Constitution *Dei Verbum* synthesized this datum when it stated that "God, who creates and conserves all things by his word (cf. *Jn* 1:3), provides constant evidence of himself in created realities".[25]

---

[23] Cf. *In Hexaemeron*, XX, 5: Opera Omnia V, Quaracchi 1891, pp. 425-426; *Breviloquium* I, 8: Opera Omnia V, Quaracchi 1891, pp. 216-217.

[24] *Itinerarium mentis in Deum*, II, 12: Opera Omnia V, Quaracchi 1891, pp. 302-303; cf. *Commentarius in librum Ecclesiastes*, Cap. 1, vers. 11; *Quaestiones*, II, 3: Opera Omnia VI, Quaracchi 1891, p. 16.

[25] SECOND VATICAN ECUMENICAL COUNCIL, Dogmatic Constitution on Divine Revelation *Dei Verbum*, 3; cf. FIRST VATICAN ECUMENICAL COUNCIL, Dogmatic Constitution on the Catholic Faith *Dei Filius*, Chap. 2, De Revelatione: DS 3004.

9.   Reality, then is born of the word, as *creatura Verbi*, and everything is called to serve the word. Creation is the setting in which the entire history of the love between God and his creation develops; hence human salvation is the reason underlying everything. Contemplating the cosmos from the perspective of salvation history, we come to realize the unique and singular position occupied by man in creation: "God created man in his own image, in the image of God he created him: male and female he created them" (*Gen* 1:27). This enables us to acknowledge fully the precious gifts received from the Creator: the value of our body, the gift of reason, freedom and conscience. Here too we discover what the philosophical tradition calls "the natural law".[26] In effect, "every human being who comes to consciousness and to responsibility has the experience of an inner call to do good"[27] and thus to avoid evil. As Saint Thomas Aquinas says, this principle is the basis of all the other precepts of the natural law.[28] Listening to the word of God leads us first and foremost to value the need to live in accordance with this law "written on human hearts" (cf. *Rom* 2:15; 7:23).[29]

[26] Cf. *Propositio* 13.

[27] INTERNATIONAL THEOLOGICAL COMMISSION, *In Search of a Universal Ethics: A New Look at the Natural Law*, Vatican City, 2009, No. 39.

[28] Cf. *Summa Theologiae*, Ia-IIae, q. 94, a. 2.

[29] Cf. PONTIFICAL BIBLICAL COMMISSION, *The Bible and Morality, Biblical Roots of Christian Conduct* (11 May 2008), Vatican City, 2008, Nos. 13, 32, 109.

Jesus Christ then gives mankind the new law, the law of the Gospel, which takes up and eminently fulfils the natural law, setting us free from the law of sin, as a result of which, as Saint Paul says, "I can will what is right, but I cannot do it" (*Rom* 7:18). It likewise enables men and women, through grace, to share in the divine life and to overcome their selfishness.[30]

The realism of the word

10.   Those who know God's word also know fully the significance of each creature. For if all things "hold together" in the one who is "before all things" (cf. *Col* 1:17), then those who build their lives on his word build in a truly sound and lasting way. The word of God makes us change our concept of realism: the realist is the one who recognizes in the word of God the foundation of all things.[31] This realism is particularly needed in our own time, when many things in which we trust for building our lives, things in which we are tempted to put our hopes, prove ephemeral. Possessions, pleasure and power show themselves sooner or later to be incapable of fulfilling the deepest yearnings of the human heart. In building our lives we need solid foundations which will

[30] Cf. INTERNATIONAL THEOLOGICAL COMMISSION, *In Search of a Universal Ethics: A New Look at the Natural Law*, Vatican City, 2009, No. 102.

[31] Cf. BENEDICT XVI, *Homily during the Celebration of Terce at the Beginning of the First General Congregation of the Synod of Bishops* (6 October 2008): AAS 100 (2008), 758-761.

endure when human certainties fail. Truly, since "for ever, O Lord, your word is firmly fixed in the heavens" and the faithfulness of the Lord "endures to all generations" (*Ps* 119:89-90), whoever builds on this word builds the house of his life on rock (cf. *Mt* 7:24). May our heart be able to say to God each day: "You are my refuge and my shield; I hope in your word" (*Ps* 119:114), and, like Saint Peter, may we entrust ourselves in our daily actions to the Lord Jesus: "At your word I will let down the nets" (*Lk* 5:5).

Christology of the word

11.   From this glimpse at all reality as the handiwork of the Blessed Trinity through the divine Word, we can understand the statement made by the author of the *Letter to the Hebrews*: "in many and various ways God spoke of old to our fathers by the prophets; but in these last days he has spoken to us by a Son, whom he appointed the heir of all things, through whom also he created the world" (1:1-2). It is very beautiful to see how the entire Old Testament already appears to us as a history in which God communicates his word: indeed, "by his covenant with Abraham (cf. *Gen* 15:18) and, through Moses, with the race of Israel (cf. *Ex* 24:8), he gained a people for himself, and to them he revealed himself in words and deeds as the one, living and true God. It was his plan that Israel might learn by experience God's ways with humanity and, by listening to the voice

of God speaking to them through the prophets, might gradually understand his ways more fully and more clearly, and make them more widely known among the nations (cf. *Ps* 21:28-29; 95:1-3; *Is* 2:1-4; *Jer* 3:17)".[32]

This "condescension" of God is accomplished surpassingly in the incarnation of the Word. The eternal Word, expressed in creation and communicated in salvation history, in Christ became a man, "born of woman" (*Gal* 4:4). Here the word finds expression not primarily in discourse, concepts or rules. Here we are set before the very person of Jesus. His unique and singular history is the definitive word which God speaks to humanity. We can see, then, why "being Christian is not the result of an ethical choice or a lofty idea, but the encounter with an event, a person, which gives life a new horizon and a definitive direction".[33] The constant renewal of this encounter and this awareness fills the hearts of believers with amazement at God's initiative, which human beings, with our own reason and imagination, could never have dreamt of. We are speaking of an unprecedented and humanly inconceivable novelty: "the word became flesh and dwelt among us" (*Jn* 1:14a). These words are no figure of speech; they point to a lived experience! Saint John, an eyewitness, tells us so: "We have

---

[32] SECOND VATICAN ECUMENICAL COUNCIL, Dogmatic Constitution on Divine Revelation *Dei Verbum*, 14.

[33] BENEDICT XVI, Encyclical Letter *Deus Caritas Est* (25 December 2005), 1: AAS 98 (2006), 217-218.

beheld his glory, glory as of the only Son from the Father, full of grace and truth" (*Jn* 1:14b). The apostolic faith testifies that the eternal Word became one of us. The *divine Word* is truly expressed in *human words*.

12.   The patristic and medieval tradition, in contemplating this "Christology of the word", employed an evocative expression: *the word was "abbreviated"*.[34] "The Fathers of the Church found in their Greek translation of the Old Testament a passage from the prophet Isaiah that Saint Paul also quotes in order to show how God's new ways had already been foretold in the Old Testament. There we read: 'The Lord made his word short, he abbreviated it' (*Is* 10:23; *Rom* 9:28) … The Son himself is the Word, the *Logos*: the eternal word became small – small enough to fit into a manger. He became a child, so that the word could be grasped by us".[35] Now the word is not simply audible; not only does it have a *voice*, now the word has a *face*, one which we can see: that of Jesus of Nazareth.[36]

Reading the Gospel accounts, we see how Jesus' own humanity appears in all its uniqueness precisely with regard to the word of God. In his perfect humanity he does the will of the

[34] "Ho Logos pachynetai (or: brachynetai)". Cf. ORIGEN, *Peri Archon*, I, 2,8: SC 252, 127-129.
[35] BENEDICT XVI, *Homily on the Solemnity of the Birth of the Lord* (24 December 2006): AAS 99 (2007), 12.
[36] Cf. *Final Message*, II, 4-6.

Father at all times; Jesus hears his voice and obeys it with his entire being; he knows the Father and he keeps his word (cf. *Jn* 8:55); he speaks to us of what the Father has told him (cf. *Jn* 12:50); I have given them the words which you gave me" (*Jn* 17:8). Jesus thus shows that he is the divine *Logos* which is given to us, but at the same time the new Adam, the true man, who unfailingly does not his own will but that of the Father. He "increased in wisdom and in stature, and in favour with God and man" (*Lk* 2:52). In a perfect way, he hears, embodies and communicates to us the word of God (cf. *Lk* 5:1).

Jesus' mission is ultimately fulfilled in the paschal mystery: here we find ourselves before the "word of the cross" (*1 Cor* 1:18). The word is muted; it becomes mortal silence, for it has "spoken" exhaustively, holding back nothing of what it had to tell us. The Fathers of the Church, in pondering this mystery, attributed to the Mother of God this touching phrase: "Wordless is the Word of the Father, who made every creature which speaks, lifeless are the eyes of the one at whose word and whose nod all living things move".[37] Here that "greater" love, the love which gives its life for its friends (cf. *Jn* 15:13), is truly shared with us.

In this great mystery Jesus is revealed as *the word of the new and everlasting covenant*: divine freedom and human freedom have definitively met

---

[37] MAXIMUS THE CONFESSOR, *Life of Mary*, No. 89: *Testi mariani del primo millennio*, 2, Rome, 1989, p. 253.

in his crucified flesh, in an indissoluble and eternally valid compact. Jesus himself, at the Last Supper, in instituting the Eucharist, had spoken of a "new and everlasting covenant" in the outpouring of his blood (cf. *Mt* 26:28; *Mk* 14:24; *Lk* 22:20), and shows himself to be the true sacrificial Lamb who brings about our definitive liberation from slavery.[38]

In the most luminous mystery of the resurrection, this silence of the word is shown in its authentic and definitive meaning. Christ, the incarnate, crucified and risen Word of God, is Lord of all things; he is the victor, the *Pantocrator*, and so all things are gathered up forever in him (cf. *Eph* 1:10). Christ is thus "the light of the world" (*Jn* 8:12), the light which "shines in the darkness" (*Jn* 1:5) and which the darkness has not overcome (cf. *Jn* 1:5). Here we come to understand fully the meaning of the words of *Psalm 119*: "Your word is a lamp to my feet and a light to my path" (v. 105); the risen Word is this definitive light to our path. From the beginning, Christians realized that in Christ the word of God is present as a person. The word of God is the true light which men and women need. In the resurrection the Son of God truly emerged as the light of the world. Now, by living with him and in him, we can live in the light.

---

[38] Cf. BENEDICT XVI, Post-Synodal Apostolic Exhortation *Sacramentum Caritatis* (22 February 2007), 9-10: AAS 99 (2007), 111-112.

13.   Here, at the heart, as it were, of the "Christology of the word", it is important to stress the unity of the divine plan in the incarnate Word: the New Testament thus presents the paschal mystery as being in accordance with the sacred Scriptures and as their deepest fulfillment. Saint Paul, in the *First Letter to the Corinthians*, states that Jesus Christ died for our sins "in accordance with the Scriptures" (15:3) and that he rose on the third day "in accordance with the Scriptures" (15:4). The Apostle thus relates the event of the Lord's death and resurrection to the history of the Old Covenant of God with his people. Indeed, he shows us that from that event history receives its inner logic and its true meaning. In the paschal mystery "the words of Scripture" are fulfilled; in other words, this death which took place "in accordance with the Scriptures" is an event containing a *logos*, an inner logic: the death of Christ testifies that the word of God became thoroughly human "flesh", human "history".[39] Similarly, the resurrection of Jesus takes place "on the third day in accordance with the Scriptures": since Jewish belief held that decay set in after the third day, the word of Scripture is fulfilled in Jesus who rises incorrupt. Thus Saint Paul, faithfully handing on the teaching of the Apostles (cf. *1 Cor* 15:3), stresses that Christ's victory over death took place through the creative power of the word of God. This divine power

[39] BENEDICT XVI, *General Audience* (15 April 2009): *L'Osservatore Romano*, 16 April 2009, p.1.

brings hope and joy: this, in a word, is the liberating content of the paschal revelation. At Easter, God reveals himself and the power of the trinitarian love which shatters the baneful powers of evil and death.

Calling to mind these essential elements of our faith, we can contemplate the profound unity in Christ between creation, the new creation and all salvation history. To use an example, we can compare the cosmos to a "book" – Galileo himself used this example – and consider it as "the work of an author who expresses himself through the 'symphony' of creation. In this symphony one finds, at a certain point, what would be called in musical terms a 'solo', a theme entrusted to a single instrument or voice which is so important that the meaning of the entire work depends on it. This 'solo' is Jesus. ... The Son of Man recapitulates in himself earth and heaven, creation and the Creator, flesh and Spirit. He is the centre of the cosmos and of history, for in him converge without confusion the author and his work".[40]

The eschatological dimension of the word of God

14.   In all of this, the Church gives voice to her awareness that with Jesus Christ she stands before the definitive word of God: he is "the first and the last" (*Rev* 1:17). He has given creation and

<hr>

[40] Id., *Homily for the Solemnity of Epiphany* (6 January 2009): *L'Osservatore Romano*, 7-8 January 2009, p. 8.

history their definitive meaning; and hence we are called to live in time and in God's creation within this eschatological rhythm of the word; "thus the Christian dispensation, since it is the new and definitive covenant, will never pass away; and no new public revelation is to be expected before the glorious manifestation of our Lord Jesus Christ (cf. *1 Tim* 6:14 and *Tit* 2:13)".[41] Indeed, as the Fathers noted during the Synod, the "uniqueness of Christianity is manifested in the event which is Jesus Christ, the culmination of revelation, the fulfilment of God's promises and the mediator of the encounter between man and God. He who 'has made God known' (*Jn* 1:18) is the one, definitive word given to mankind".[42] Saint John of the Cross expresses this truth magnificently: "Since he has given us his Son, his only word (for he possesses no other), he spoke everything at once in this sole word – and he has no more to say... because what he spoke before to the prophets in parts, he has spoken all at once by giving us this All who is his Son. Any person questioning God or desiring some vision or revelation would be guilty not only of foolish behaviour but also of offending him, by not fixing his eyes entirely on Christ and by living with the desire for some other novelty".[43]

---

[41] SECOND VATICAN ECUMENICAL COUNCIL, Dogmatic Constitution on Divine Revelation *Dei Verbum*, 4.

[42] *Propositio* 4.

[43] SAINT JOHN OF THE CROSS, *Ascent of Mount Carmel*, II, 22.

Consequently the Synod pointed to the need to "help the faithful to distinguish the word of God from private revelations"[44] whose role "is not to 'complete' Christ's definitive revelation, but to help live more fully by it in a certain period of history".[45] The value of private revelations is essentially different from that of the one public revelation: the latter demands faith; in it God himself speaks to us through human words and the mediation of the living community of the Church. The criterion for judging the truth of a private revelation is its orientation to Christ himself. If it leads us away from him, then it certainly does not come from the Holy Spirit, who guides us more deeply into the Gospel, and not away from it. Private revelation is an aid to this faith, and it demonstrates its credibility precisely because it refers back to the one public revelation. Ecclesiastical approval of a private revelation essentially means that its message contains nothing contrary to faith and morals; it is licit to make it public and the faithful are authorized to give to it their prudent adhesion. A private revelation can introduce new emphases, give rise to new forms of piety, or deepen older ones. It can have a certain prophetic character (cf. *1 Th* 5:19-21) and can be a valuable aid for better understanding and living the Gospel at a certain time; consequently it should not be treated lightly. It is a help which

[44] *Propositio* 47.
[45] *Catechism of the Catholic Church*, 67.

is proffered, but its use is not obligatory. In any event, it must be a matter of nourishing faith, hope and love, which are for everyone the permanent path of salvation.[46]

The word of God and the Holy Spirit

15.   After reflecting on God's final and definitive word to the world, we need now to mention the mission of the Holy Spirit in relation to the divine word. In fact there can be no authentic understanding of Christian revelation apart from the activity of the Paraclete. This is due to the fact that God's self-communication always involves the relationship of the Son and the Holy Spirit, whom Irenaeus of Lyons refers to as "the two hands of the Father".[47] Sacred Scripture itself speaks of the presence of the Holy Spirit in salvation history and particularly in the life of Jesus: he was conceived of the Virgin Mary by the power of the Holy Spirit (cf. *Mt* 1:18; *Lk* 1:35); at the beginning of his public mission, on the banks of the Jordan, he sees the Holy Spirit descend on him in the form of a dove (cf. *Mt* 3:16); in this same Spirit Jesus acts, speaks and rejoices (cf. *Lk* 10:21); and in the Spirit he offers himself up (cf. *Heb* 9:14). As his mission draws to an end, according to the account of Saint John, Jesus

[46] Cf. CONGREGATION FOR THE DOCTRINE OF THE FAITH, *The Message of Fatima* (26 June 2000): *Enchiridion Vaticanum* 19, Nos. 974-1021.

[47] *Adversus Haereses*, IV, 7, 4: PG 7, 992-993; V, 1, 3: PG 7, 1123; V, 6, 1: PG 7, 1137; V, 28, 4: PG 7, 1200.

himself clearly relates the giving of his life to the sending of the Spirit upon those who belong to him (cf. *Jn* 16:7). The Risen Jesus, bearing in his flesh the signs of the passion, then pours out the Spirit (cf. *Jn* 20:22), making his disciples sharers in his own mission (cf. *Jn* 20:21). The Holy Spirit was to teach the disciples all things and bring to their remembrance all that Christ had said (cf. *Jn* 14:26), since he, the Spirit of Truth (cf. *Jn* 15:26) will guide the disciples into all the truth (cf. *Jn* 16:13). Finally, in the *Acts of the Apostles*, we read that the Spirit descended on the Twelve gathered in prayer with Mary on the day of Pentecost (cf. 2:1-4), and impelled them to take up the mission of proclaiming to all peoples the Good News.[48]

The word of God is thus expressed in human words thanks to the working of the Holy Spirit. The missions of the Son and the Holy Spirit are inseparable and constitute a single economy of salvation. The same Spirit who acts in the incarnation of the Word in the womb of the Virgin Mary is the Spirit who guides Jesus throughout his mission and is promised to the disciples. The same Spirit who spoke through the prophets sustains and inspires the Church in her task of proclaiming the word of God and in the preaching of the Apostles; finally, it is this Spirit who inspires the authors of sacred Scripture.

---

[48] Cf. BENEDICT XVI, Post-Synodal Apostolic Exhortation *Sacramentum Caritatis* (22 February 2007), 12: AAS 99 (2007), 113-114.

16. Conscious of this pneumatological horizon, the Synod Fathers highlighted the importance of the Holy Spirit's work in the life of the Church and in the hearts of believers in relation to sacred Scripture:[49] without the efficacious working of the "Spirit of Truth" (*Jn* 14:16), the words of the Lord cannot be understood. As Saint Irenaeus states: "Those who do not share in the Spirit do not draw from the bosom of their mother [the Church] the food of life; they receive nothing from the purest fountain that flows from the body of Christ".[50] Just as the word of God comes to us in the body of Christ, in his Eucharistic body and in the body of the Scriptures, through the working of the Holy Spirit, so too it can only be truly received and understood through that same Spirit.

The great writers of the Christian tradition speak unanimously of the place of the Holy Spirit in the relationship which believers are to have with the Scriptures. Saint John Chrysostom states that Scripture "needs the revelation of the Spirit, so that by discovering the true meaning of the things enclosed therein, we can reap abundant benefits".[51] Saint Jerome is likewise firmly convinced that "we cannot come to an understanding of Scripture without the assistance of the Holy Spirit who inspired it".[52] Saint Gregory the Great nicely emphasizes the work of the Spirit in the

---

[49] Cf. *Propositio* 5.
[50] *Adversus Haereses*, III, 24, 1: PG 7, 966.
[51] *Homiliae in Genesim*, XXII, 1: PG 53, 175.
[52] *Epistula* 120, 10: CSEL 55, 500-506.

formation and interpretation of the Bible: "He himself created the words of the holy Testaments, he himself revealed their meaning".[53] Richard of Saint Victor points out that we need "the eyes of doves", enlightened and taught by the Spirit, in order to understand the sacred text.[54]

Here too I would like to emphasize the very significant witness to the relationship between the Holy Spirit and Scripture which we find in the texts of the liturgy, where the word of God is proclaimed, heard and explained to the faithful. We find a witness to this in the ancient prayers which in the form of an epiclesis invoke the Spirit before the proclamation of the readings: "Send your Paraclete Spirit into our hearts and make us understand the Scriptures which he has inspired; and grant that I may interpret them worthily, so that the faithful assembled here may profit thereby". We also find prayers which, at the end of the homily, again ask God to send the gift of the Spirit upon the faithful: "God our Saviour... we implore you for this people: send upon them the Holy Spirit; may the Lord Jesus come to visit them, speak to the minds of all, dispose their hearts to faith and lead our souls to you, God of mercies".[55] This makes it clear that we cannot

[53] *Homiliae in Ezechielem*, I, VII, 17: CC 142, p. 94.

[54] "Oculi ergo devotae animae sunt columbarum quia sensus eius per Spiritum sanctum sunt illuminati et edocti, spiritualia sapientes. Nunc quidem aperitur animae talis sensus, ut intellegat Scripturas": RICHARD OF SAINT VICTOR, *Explicatio in Cantica Canticorum*, 15: PL 196, 450B and D.

[55] *Sacramentarium Serapionis* II (XX): *Didascalia et Constitutiones Apostolorum*, ed F.X. FUNK, II, Paderborn, 1906, p. 161.

come to understand the meaning of the word unless we are open to the working of the Paraclete in the Church and in the hearts of believers.

Tradition and Scripture

17.   In reaffirming the profound connection between the Holy Spirit and the word of God, we have also laid the basis for an understanding of the significance and the decisive value of the living Tradition and the sacred Scriptures in the Church. Indeed, since God "so loved the world that he gave his only Son" (*Jn* 3:16), the divine word, spoken in time, is bestowed and "consigned" to the Church in a definitive way, so that the proclamation of salvation can be communicated effectively in every time and place. As the Dogmatic Constitution *Dei Verbum* reminds us, Jesus Christ himself "commanded the Apostles to preach the Gospel – promised beforehand by the prophets, fulfilled in his own person and promulgated by his own lips – to all as the source of all saving truth and moral law, communicating God's gifts to them. This was faithfully carried out; it was carried out by the Apostles who handed on, by oral preaching, by their example, by their ordinances, what they themselves had received – whether from the lips of Christ, from his way of life and his works, or by coming to know it through the prompting of the Holy Spirit; it was carried out by those Apostles and others as-

sociated with them who, under the inspiration of the same Holy Spirit, committed the message of salvation to writing".[56]

The Second Vatican Council also states that this Tradition of apostolic origin is a living and dynamic reality: it "makes progress in the Church, with the help of the Holy Spirit"; yet not in the sense that it changes in its truth, which is perennial. Rather, "there is a growth in insight into the realities and the words that are being passed on", through contemplation and study, with the understanding granted by deeper spiritual experience and by the "preaching of those who, on succeeding to the office of bishop, have received the sure charism of truth".[57]

The living Tradition is essential for enabling the Church to grow through time in the understanding of the truth revealed in the Scriptures; indeed, "by means of the same tradition, the full canon of the sacred books is known to the Church and the holy Scriptures themselves are more thoroughly understood and constantly made effective in the Church".[58] Ultimately, it is the living Tradition of the Church which makes us adequately understand sacred Scripture as the word of God. Although the word of God precedes and exceeds sacred Scripture, nonetheless Scripture, as in-

---

[56] SECOND VATICAN ECUMENICAL COUNCIL, Dogmatic Constitution on Divine Revelation *Dei Verbum*, 7.

[57] *Ibid.*, 8.

[58] *Ibid.*

spired by God, contains the divine word (cf. *2 Tim* 3:16) "in an altogether singular way".[59]

18.   We see clearly, then, how important it is for the People of God to be properly taught and trained to approach the sacred Scriptures in relation to the Church's living Tradition, and to recognize in them the very word of God. Fostering such an approach in the faithful is very important from the standpoint of the spiritual life. Here it might be helpful to recall the analogy drawn by the Fathers of the Church between the word of God which became "flesh" and the word which became a "book".[60] The Dogmatic Constitution *Dei Verbum* takes up this ancient tradition which holds, as Saint Ambrose says,[61] that "the body of the Son is the Scripture which we have received", and declares that "the words of God, expressed in human language, are in every way like human speech, just as the word of the eternal Father, when he took on himself the weak flesh of human beings, became like them".[62] When understood in this way, sacred Scripture presents itself to us, in the variety of its many forms and content, as a single reality. Indeed, "through all the words of sacred Scripture, God speaks only one single word, his one utterance, in whom he

[59]   Cf. *Propositio* 3.
[60]   Cf. *Final Message* II, 5.
[61]   *Expositio Evangelii secundum Lucam*, 6, 33: PL 15, 1677.
[62]   SECOND VATICAN ECUMENICAL COUNCIL, Dogmatic Constitution on Divine Revelation *Dei Verbum*, 13.

expresses himself completely (cf. *Heb* 1:1-3)".[63] Saint Augustine had already made the point clearly: "Remember that one alone is the discourse of God which unfolds in all sacred Scripture, and one alone is the word which resounds on the lips of all the holy writers".[64]

In short, by the work of the Holy Spirit and under the guidance of the magisterium, the Church hands on to every generation all that has been revealed in Christ. The Church lives in the certainty that her Lord, who spoke in the past, continues today to communicate his word in her living Tradition and in sacred Scripture. Indeed, the word of God is given to us in sacred Scripture as an inspired testimony to revelation; together with the Church's living Tradition, it constitutes the supreme rule of faith.[65]

Sacred Scripture, inspiration and truth

19.   A key concept for understanding the sacred text as the word of God in human words is certainly that of *inspiration*. Here too we can suggest an analogy: as the word of God became flesh by the power of the Holy Spirit in the womb of the Virgin Mary, so sacred Scripture is born from the

---

[63] *Catechism of the Catholic Church*, 102; Cf. also RUPERT OF DEUTZ, *De Operibus Spiritus Sancti*, I, 6: SC 131:72-74.

[64] *Enarrationes in Psalmos*, 103, IV, 1: PL 37, 1378. Similar statements in ORIGEN, *In Iohannem* V, 5-6: SC 120, pp. 380-384.

[65] Cf. SECOND VATICAN ECUMENICAL COUNCIL, Dogmatic Constitution on Divine Revelation *Dei Verbum*, 21.

womb of the Church by the power of the same Spirit. Sacred Scripture is "the word of God set down in writing under the inspiration of the Holy Spirit".[66] In this way one recognizes the full importance of the human author who wrote the inspired texts and, at the same time, God himself as the true author.

As the Synod Fathers affirmed, the theme of inspiration is clearly decisive for an adequate approach to the Scriptures and their correct interpretation,[67] which for its part is to be done in the same Spirit in whom the sacred texts were written.[68] Whenever our awareness of its inspiration grows weak, we risk reading Scripture as an object of historical curiosity and not as the work of the Holy Spirit in which we can hear the Lord himself speak and recognize his presence in history.

The Synod Fathers also stressed the link between the theme of inspiration and that of the *truth of the Scriptures*.[69] A deeper study of the process of inspiration will doubtless lead to a greater understanding of the truth contained in the sacred books. As the Council's teaching states in this regard, the inspired books teach the truth: "since, therefore, all that the inspired authors, or sacred writers, affirm should be regarded as affirmed by

[66] *Ibid.*, 9.
[67] Cf. *Propositiones* 5 and 12.
[68] Cf. SECOND VATICAN ECUMENICAL COUNCIL, Dogmatic Constitution on Divine Revelation *Dei Verbum*, 12.
[69] Cf. *Propositio* 12.

the Holy Spirit, we must acknowledge that the books of Scripture firmly, faithfully and without error, teach that truth which God, for the sake of our salvation, wished to see confided to the sacred Scriptures. Thus, 'all scripture is inspired by God and is useful for teaching, for reproof, for correction and for training in righteousness, so that the man of God may be proficient, equipped for every good work' (*2 Tim* 3:16-17, Greek)".[70]

Certainly theological reflection has always considered inspiration and truth as two key concepts for an ecclesial hermeneutic of the sacred Scriptures. Nonetheless, one must acknowledge the need today for a fuller and more adequate study of these realities, in order better to respond to the need to interpret the sacred texts in accordance with their nature. Here I would express my fervent hope that research in this field will progress and bear fruit both for biblical science and for the spiritual life of the faithful.

God the Father, source and origin of the word

20.   The economy of revelation has its beginning and origin in God the Father. By his word "the heavens were made, and all their host by the breath of his mouth" (*Ps* 33:6). It is he who has given us "the light of the knowledge of the glory of God in the face of Christ" (*2 Cor* 4:6; cf. *Mt* 16:17; *Lk* 9:29).

---

[70] SECOND VATICAN ECUMENICAL COUNCIL, Dogmatic Constitution on Divine Revelation *Dei Verbum*, 11.

In the Son, "*Logos* made flesh" (cf. *Jn* 1:14), who came to accomplish the will of the one who sent him (cf. *Jn* 4:34), God, the source of revelation, reveals himself as Father and brings to completion the divine pedagogy which had previously been carried out through the words of the prophets and the wondrous deeds accomplished in creation and in the history of his people and all mankind. The revelation of God the Father culminates in the Son's gift of the Paraclete (cf. *Jn* 14:16), the Spirit of the Father and the Son, who guides us "into all the truth" (*Jn* 16:13).

All God's promises find their "yes" in Jesus Christ (cf. *2 Cor* 1:20). Men and women are thus enabled to set out on the way that leads to the Father (cf. *Jn* 14:6), so that in the end "God may be everything to everyone" (*1 Cor* 15:28).

21.   As the cross of Christ demonstrates, God also speaks by his silence. The silence of God, the experience of the distance of the almighty Father, is a decisive stage in the earthly journey of the Son of God, the incarnate Word. Hanging from the wood of the cross, he lamented the suffering caused by that silence: "My God, my God, why have you forsaken me?" (*Mk* 15:34; *Mt* 27:46). Advancing in obedience to his very last breath, in the obscurity of death, Jesus called upon the Father. He commended himself to him at the moment of passage, through death, to eternal life: "Father, into your hands I commend my spirit" (*Lk* 23:46).

This experience of Jesus reflects the situation of all those who, having heard and acknowledged God's word, must also confront his silence. This has been the experience of countless saints and mystics, and even today is part of the journey of many believers. God's silence prolongs his earlier words. In these moments of darkness, he speaks through the mystery of his silence. Hence, in the dynamic of Christian revelation, silence appears as an important expression of the word of God.

Our Response To The God Who Speaks

Called to the covenant with God

22.   By emphasizing the many forms of the word, we have been able to contemplate the number of ways in which God speaks to and encounters men and women, making himself known in dialogue. Certainly, as the Synod Fathers stated, "dialogue, when we are speaking of revelation, entails the *primacy* of the word of God addressed to man".[71] The mystery of the Covenant expresses this relationship between God who calls man with his word, and man who responds, albeit making clear that it is not a matter of a meeting of two peers; what we call the Old and New Covenant is not a contract between two equal parties, but a pure gift of God. By this gift of his love God bridges every distance and truly makes us his "partners", in or-

[71] *Propositio* 4.

der to bring about the nuptial mystery of the love between Christ and the Church. In this vision every man and woman appears as someone to whom the word speaks, challenges and calls to enter this dialogue of love through a free response. Each of us is thus enabled by God to *hear and respond* to his word. We were created in the word and we live in the word; we cannot understand ourselves unless we are open to this dialogue. The word of God discloses the filial and relational nature of human existence. We are indeed called by grace to be conformed to Christ, the Son of the Father, and, in him, to be transformed.

God hears us and responds to our questions

23.   In this dialogue with God we come to understand ourselves and we discover an answer to our heart's deepest questions. The word of God in fact is not inimical to us; it does not stifle our authentic desires, but rather illuminates them, purifies them and brings them to fulfilment. How important it is for our time to discover that *God alone responds to the yearning present in the heart of every man and woman!* Sad to say, in our days, and in the West, there is a widespread notion that God is extraneous to people's lives and problems, and that his very presence can be a threat to human autonomy. Yet the entire economy of salvation demonstrates that God speaks and acts in history for our good and our integral salvation. Thus it is decisive, from the pastoral standpoint, to present the

word of God in its capacity to enter into dialogue with the everyday problems which people face. Jesus himself says that he came that we might have life in abundance (cf. *Jn* 10:10). Consequently, we need to make every effort to share the word of God as an openness to our problems, a response to our questions, a broadening of our values and the fulfilment of our aspirations. The Church's pastoral activity needs to bring out clearly how God listens to our need and our plea for help. As Saint Bonaventure says in the *Breviloquium*: "The fruit of sacred Scripture is not any fruit whatsoever, but the very fullness of eternal happiness. Sacred Scripture is the book containing the words of eternal life, so that we may not only believe in, but also possess eternal life, in which we will see and love, and all our desires will be fulfilled".[72]

In dialogue with God through his words

24.   The word of God draws each of us into a conversation with the Lord: the God who speaks teaches us how to speak to him. Here we naturally think of the *Book of Psalms*, where God gives us words to speak to him, to place our lives before him, and thus to make life itself a path to God.[73] In the Psalms we find expressed every possible human feeling set masterfully in the sight of God;

[72] *Prol*: Opera Omnia V, Quaracchi 1891, pp. 201-202.
[73] Cf. BENEDICT XVI, *Address to Representatives of the World of Culture at the "Collège des Bernardins" in Paris* (12 September 2008): AAS 100 (2008), 721-730.

joy and pain, distress and hope, fear and trepidation: here all find expression. Along with the Psalms we think too of the many other passages of sacred Scripture which express our turning to God in intercessory prayer (cf. *Ex* 33:12-16), in exultant songs of victory (cf. *Ex* 15) or in sorrow at the difficulties experienced in carrying out our mission (cf. *Jer* 20:7-18). In this way our word to God becomes God's word, thus confirming the dialogical nature of all Christian revelation,[74] and our whole existence becomes a dialogue with the God who speaks and listens, who calls us and gives direction to our lives. Here the word of God reveals that our entire life is under the divine call.[75]

The word of God and faith

25. "'The obedience of faith' (*Rom* 16:26; cf. *Rom* 1:5; *2 Cor* 10:5-6) must be our response to God who reveals. By faith one freely commits oneself entirely to God, making 'the full submission of intellect and will to God who reveals' and willingly assenting to the revelation given by God".[76] In these words the Dogmatic Constitution *Dei Verbum* gave precise expression to the stance which we must have with regard to God. *The proper human response to the God who speaks is faith.* Here we see clearly that "in order to accept

---

[74] Cf. *Propositio* 4.

[75] Cf. *Relatio post disceptationem*, 12.

[76] SECOND VATICAN ECUMENICAL COUNCIL, Dogmatic Constitution on Divine Revelation *Dei Verbum*, 5.

revelation, man must open his mind and heart to the working of the Holy Spirit who enables him to understand the word of God present in the sacred Scriptures".[77] It is the preaching of the divine word, in fact, which gives rise to faith, whereby we give our heartfelt assent to the truth which has been revealed to us and we commit ourselves entirely to Christ: "faith comes from what is heard, and what is heard comes from the word of Christ" (*Rom* 10:17). The whole history of salvation progressively demonstrates this profound bond between the word of God and the faith which arises from an encounter with Christ. Faith thus takes shape as an encounter with a person to whom we entrust our whole life. Christ Jesus remains present today in history, in his body which is the Church; for this reason our act of faith is at once both personal and ecclesial.

Sin as a refusal to hear the word of God

26.   The word of God also inevitably reveals the tragic possibility that human freedom can withdraw from this covenant dialogue with God for which we were created. The divine word also discloses the sin that lurks in the human heart. Quite frequently in both the Old and in the New Testament, we find sin described as a *refusal to hear the word*, as a *breaking of the covenant* and thus as being closed to God who calls us to communion with

[77] *Propositio* 4.

himself.[78] Sacred Scripture shows how man's sin is essentially disobedience and refusal to hear. The radical obedience of Jesus even to his death on the cross (cf. *Phil* 2:8) completely unmasks this sin. His obedience brings about the New Covenant between God and man, and grants us the possibility of reconciliation. Jesus was sent by the Father as a sacrifice of atonement for our sins and for those of the whole world (cf. *1 Jn* 2:2; 4:10; *Heb* 7:27). We are thus offered the merciful possibility of redemption and the start of a new life in Christ. For this reason it is important that the faithful be taught to acknowledge that the root of sin lies in the refusal to hear the word of the Lord, and to accept in Jesus, the Word of God, the forgiveness which opens us to salvation.

Mary, "Mother of God's Word" and "Mother of Faith"

27. The Synod Fathers declared that the basic aim of the Twelfth Assembly was "to renew the Church's faith in the word of God". To do so, we need to look to the one in whom the interplay between the word of God and faith was brought to perfection, that is, to the Virgin Mary, "who by her 'yes' to the word of the covenant and her mission, perfectly fulfills the divine vocation of humanity".[79] The human reality created through

---

[78] For example: *Dt* 28:1-2,15,45; 32:1; among the prophets, see: *Jer* 7:22-28; *Ez* 2:8; 3:10; 6:3; 13:2; up to the latest: cf. *Zech* 3:8. For Saint Paul, cf. *Rom* 10:14-18; *1 Th* 2:13.

[79] *Propositio* 55.

the word finds its most perfect image in Mary's obedient faith. From the Annunciation to Pentecost she appears as a woman completely open to the will of God. She is the Immaculate Conception, the one whom God made "full of grace" (cf. *Lk* 1:28) and unconditionally docile to his word (cf. *Lk* 1:38). Her obedient faith shapes her life at every moment before God's plan. A Virgin ever attentive to God's word, she lives completely attuned to that word; she treasures in her heart the events of her Son, piecing them together as if in a single mosaic (cf. *Lk* 2:19,51).[80]

In our day the faithful need to be helped to see more clearly the link between Mary of Nazareth and the faith-filled hearing of God's word. I would encourage scholars as well to study the relationship between *Mariology and the theology of the word*. This could prove most beneficial both for the spiritual life and for theological and biblical studies. Indeed, what the understanding of the faith has enabled us to know about Mary stands at the heart of Christian truth. The incarnation of the word cannot be conceived apart from the freedom of this young woman who by her assent decisively cooperated with the entrance of the eternal into time. Mary is the image of the Church in attentive hearing of the word of God, which took flesh in her. Mary also symbolizes

---

[80] Cf. BENEDICT XVI, Post-Synodal Apostolic Exhortation *Sacramentum Caritatis* (22 February 2007), 33: AAS 99 (2007), 132-133.

openness to God and others; an active listening which interiorizes and assimilates, one in which the word becomes a way of life.

28.   Here I would like to mention Mary's familiarity with the word of God. This is clearly evident in the *Magnificat*. There we see in some sense how she identifies with the word, enters into it; in this marvellous canticle of faith, the Virgin sings the praises of the Lord in his own words: "The *Magnificat* – a portrait, so to speak, of her soul – is entirely woven from threads of Holy Scripture, threads drawn from the word of God. Here we see how completely at home Mary is with the word of God, with ease she moves in and out of it. She speaks and thinks with the word of God; the word of God becomes her word, and her word issues from the word of God. Here we see how her thoughts are attuned to the thoughts of God, how her will is one with the will of God. Since Mary is completely imbued with the word of God, she is able to become the Mother of the Word Incarnate".[81]

Furthermore, in looking to the Mother of God, we see how God's activity in the world always engages our freedom, because through faith the divine word transforms us. Our apostolic and pastoral work can never be effective unless we learn from Mary how to be shaped by the working of God within us: "devout and loving atten-

[81] ID., Encyclical Letter *Deus Caritas Est* (25 December 2005), 41: AAS 98 (2006), 251.

tion to the figure of Mary as the model and archetype of the Church's faith is of capital importance for bringing about in our day a concrete paradigm shift in the Church's relation with the word, both in prayerful listening and in generous commitment to mission and proclamation".[82]

As we contemplate in the Mother of God a life totally shaped by the word, we realize that we too are called to enter into the mystery of faith, whereby Christ comes to dwell in our lives. Every Christian believer, Saint Ambrose reminds us, in some way interiorly conceives and gives birth to the word of God: even though there is only one Mother of Christ in the flesh, in the faith Christ is the progeny of us all.[83] Thus, what took place for Mary can daily take place in each of us, in the hearing of the word and in the celebration of the sacraments.

THE INTERPRETATION OF SACRED SCRIPTURE IN THE CHURCH

The Church as the primary setting for biblical hermeneutics

29.   Another major theme that emerged during the Synod, to which I would now like to draw attention, is the *interpretation of sacred Scripture in the Church*. The intrinsic link between the word and faith makes clear that authentic biblical herme-

---

[82] *Propositio* 55.
[83] Cf. *Expositio Evangelii secundum Lucam*, 2, 19: PL 15, 1559-1560.

neutics can only be had within the faith of the Church, which has its paradigm in Mary's *fiat*. Saint Bonaventure states that without faith there is no key to throw open the sacred text: "This is the knowledge of Jesus Christ, from whom, as from a fountain, flow forth the certainty and the understanding of all sacred Scripture. Therefore it is impossible for anyone to attain to knowledge of that truth unless he first have infused faith in Christ, which is the lamp, the gate and the foundation of all Scripture".[84] And Saint Thomas Aquinas, citing Saint Augustine, insists that "the letter, even that of the Gospel, would kill, were there not the inward grace of healing faith".[85]

Here we can point to a fundamental criterion of biblical hermeneutics: *the primary setting for scriptural interpretation is the life of the Church.* This is not to uphold the ecclesial context as an extrinsic rule to which exegetes must submit, but rather is something demanded by the very nature of the Scriptures and the way they gradually came into being. "Faith traditions formed the living context for the literary activity of the authors of sacred Scripture. Their insertion into this context also involved a sharing in both the liturgical and external life of the communities, in their intellectual world, in their culture and in the ups and downs of their shared history. In like manner, the interpretation

---

[84] *Breviloquium, Prol.*: Opera Omnia, V, Quaracchi 1891, pp. 201-202.

[85] *Summa Theologiae*, Ia-IIae, q. 106, art. 2.

of sacred Scripture requires full participation on the part of exegetes in the life and faith of the believing community of their own time".[86] Consequently, "since sacred Scripture must be read and interpreted in the light of the same Spirit through whom it was written",[87] exegetes, theologians and the whole people of God must approach it as what it really is, the word of God conveyed to us through human words (cf. *1 Th* 2:13). This is a constant datum implicit in the Bible itself: "No prophecy of scripture is a matter of one's own interpretation, because no prophecy ever came by the impulse of man, but men moved by the Holy Spirit spoke from God" (*2 Pet* 1:20-21). Moreover, it is the faith of the Church that recognizes in the Bible the word of God; as Saint Augustine memorably put it: "I would not believe the Gospel, had not the authority of the Catholic Church led me to do so".[88] The Holy Spirit, who gives life to the Church, enables us to interpret the Scriptures authoritatively. The Bible is the Church's book, and its essential place in the Church's life gives rise to its genuine interpretation.

30.   Saint Jerome recalls that we can never read Scripture simply on our own. We come up against

---

[86] PONTIFICAL BIBLICAL COMMISSION, *The Interpretation of the Bible in the Church* (15 April 1993), III, A, 3: *Enchiridion Vaticanum* 13, No. 3035.
[87] SECOND VATICAN ECUMENICAL COUNCIL, Dogmatic Constitution on Divine Revelation *Dei Verbum*, 12.
[88] *Contra epistulam Manichaei quam vocant fundamenti*, V, 6: PL 42, 176.

too many closed doors and we slip too easily into error. The Bible was written by the People of God for the People of God, under the inspiration of the Holy Spirit. Only in this communion with the People of God can we truly enter as a "we" into the heart of the truth that God himself wishes to convey to us.[89] Jerome, for whom "ignorance of the Scriptures is ignorance of Christ",[90] states that the ecclesial dimension of biblical interpretation is not a requirement imposed from without: the Book is the very voice of the pilgrim People of God, and only within the faith of this People are we, so to speak, attuned to understand sacred Scripture. An authentic interpretation of the Bible must always be in harmony with the faith of the Catholic Church. He thus wrote to a priest: "Remain firmly attached to the traditional doctrine that you have been taught, so that you may exhort according to sound doctrine and confound those who contradict it".[91]

Approaches to the sacred text that prescind from faith might suggest interesting elements on the level of textual structure and form, but would inevitably prove merely preliminary and structurally incomplete efforts. As the Pontifical Biblical Commission, echoing an accepted principle of modern hermeneutics, has stated: "access to a proper understanding of biblical texts is only

---

[89] Cf. BENEDICT XVI, *General Audience* (14 November 2007): *Insegnamenti* III 2 (2007), 586-591.

[90] *Commentariorum in Isaiam libri, Prol.*: PL 24, 17.

[91] *Epistula* 52:7: CSEL 54, p. 426.

granted to the person who has an affinity with what the text is saying on the basis of life experience".[92] All this brings out more clearly the relationship between the spiritual life and scriptural hermeneutics. "As the reader matures in the life of the Spirit, so there grows also his or her capacity to understand the realities of which the Bible speaks".[93] The intensity of an authentic ecclesial experience can only lead to the growth of genuine understanding in faith where the Scriptures are concerned; conversely, reading the Scriptures in faith leads to growth in ecclesial life itself. Here we can see once again the truth of the celebrated dictum of Saint Gregory the Great: "The divine words grow together with the one who reads them".[94] Listening to the word of God introduces and increases ecclesial communion with all those who walk by faith.

"The soul of sacred theology"

31. "The study of the sacred page should be, as it were, the very soul of theology":[95] this quota-

---

[92] PONTIFICAL BIBLICAL COMMISSION, *The Interpretation of the Bible in the Church* (15 April 1993), II, A, 2: *Enchiridion Vaticanum* 13, No. 2988.

[93] *Ibid.*, II, A, 2: *Enchiridion Vaticanum* 13, No. 2991.

[94] *Homiliae in Ezechielem* I, VII, 8: PL 76, 843D.

[95] SECOND VATICAN ECUMENICAL COUNCIL, Dogmatic Constitution on Divine Revelation *Dei Verbum*, 24; cf. LEO XIII, Encyclical Letter *Providentissimus Deus* (18 November 1893), Pars II, sub fine: ASS 26 (1893-94), 269-292; BENEDICT XV, Encyclical Letter *Spiritus Paraclitus* (15 September 1920), Pars III: AAS 12 (1920), 385-422.

tion from the Dogmatic Constitution *Dei Verbum* has become increasingly familiar over the years. Theological and exegetical scholarship, in the period after the Second Vatican Council, made frequent reference to this expression as symbolic of the renewed interest in sacred Scripture. The Twelfth Assembly of the Synod of Bishops also frequently alluded to this well-known phrase in order to express the relationship between historical research and a hermeneutic of faith where the sacred text is concerned. The Fathers acknowledged with joy that study of the word of God in the Church has grown in recent decades, and they expressed *heartfelt gratitude to the many exegetes and theologians* who with dedication, commitment and competence continue to make an essential contribution to the deeper understanding of the meaning of the Scriptures, as they address the complex issues facing biblical studies in our day.[96] *Sincere gratitude was also expressed to the members of the Pontifical Biblical Commission*, past and present, who in close collaboration with the Congregation for the Doctrine of the Faith continue to offer their expertise in the examination of particular questions raised by the study of sacred Scripture. The Synod likewise felt a need to look into the present state of biblical studies and their standing within the field of theology. The pastoral effectiveness of the Church's activity and the spiritual life of the faithful depend to a great extent on the fruit-

[96] Cf. *Propositio* 26.

fulness of the relationship between exegesis and theology. For this reason, I consider it important to take up some reflections that emerged in the discussion of this topic during the Synod sessions.

The development of biblical studies and the Church's magisterium

32.   Before all else, we need to acknowledge the benefits that historical-critical exegesis and other recently-developed methods of textual analysis have brought to the life of the Church.[97] For the Catholic understanding of sacred Scripture, attention to such methods is indispensable, linked as it is to the realism of the Incarnation: "This necessity is a consequence of the Christian principle formulated in the Gospel of John 1:14: *Verbum caro factum est*. The historical fact is a constitutive dimension of the Christian faith. The history of salvation is not mythology, but a true history, and it should thus be studied with the methods of serious historical research".[98] The study of the Bible requires a knowledge of these methods of enquiry and their suitable application. While it is true that scholarship has come to a much greater appreciation of their importance in the modern period, albeit not everywhere to the same degree,

---

[97] Cf. PONTIFICAL BIBLICAL COMMISSION, *The Interpretation of the Bible in the Church* (15 April 1993), A-B: *Enchiridion Vaticanum* 13, Nos. 2846-3150.

[98] BENEDICT XVI, *Intervention in the Fourteenth General Congregation of the Synod* (14 October 2008): *Insegnamenti* IV, 2 (2008), 492; cf. *Propositio* 25.

nonetheless the sound ecclesial tradition has always demonstrated a love for the study of the "letter". Here we need but recall the monastic culture which is the ultimate foundation of European culture; at its root lies a concern for the word. The desire for God includes love for the word in all its dimensions: "because in the word of the Bible God comes to us and we to him, we must learn to penetrate the secret of language, to understand it in its structure and its mode of expression. Thus, because of the search for God, the secular sciences which lead to a greater understanding of language became important".[99]

33. The Church's living magisterium, which is charged with "giving an authentic interpretation of the word of God, whether in its written form or in the form of tradition",[100] intervened in a prudent and balanced way regarding the correct response to the introduction of new methods of historical analysis. I think in particular of the Encyclicals *Providentissimus Deus* of Pope Leo XIII and *Divino Afflante Spiritu* of Pope Pius XII. My venerable predecessor John Paul II recalled the importance of these documents on the centenary and the fiftieth anniversary respectively of their promulgation.[101] Pope Leo XIII's inter-

[99] ID., *Address to Representatives of the World of Culture at the "Collège des Bernardins" in Paris* (12 September 2008): AAS 100 (2008), 722-723.
[100] SECOND VATICAN ECUMENICAL COUNCIL, Dogmatic Constitution on Divine Revelation *Dei Verbum*, 10.
[101] Cf. JOHN PAUL II, *Address for the Celebration of the Cen-*

vention had the merit of protecting the Catholic interpretation of the Bible from the inroads of rationalism, without, however, seeking refuge in a spiritual meaning detached from history. Far from shunning scientific criticism, the Church was wary only of "preconceived opinions that claim to be based on science, but which in reality surreptitiously cause science to depart from its domain".[102] Pope Pius XII, on the other hand, was faced with attacks on the part of those who proposed a so-called mystical exegesis which rejected any form of scientific approach. The Encyclical *Divino Afflante Spiritu* was careful to avoid any hint of a dichotomy between "scientific exegesis" for use in apologetics and "spiritual interpretation meant for internal use"; rather it affirmed both the "theological significance of the literal sense, methodically defined" and the fact that "determining the spiritual sense … belongs itself to the realm of exegetical science".[103] In this way, both documents rejected "a split between the human and the divine, between scientific research and respect for the faith, between the literal sense and the spiritual sense".[104] This balance was subsequently maintained by the 1993 document of the Pontifical Biblical Commission: "in their work of

tenary of the Encyclical Providentissimus Deus *and the Fiftieth Anniversary of the Encyclical* Divino Afflante Spiritu (23 April 1993): AAS 86 (1994), 232-243.
    [102] *Ibid.*, 4: AAS 86 (1994), 235.
    [103] *Ibid.*, 5: AAS 86 (1994), 235.
    [104] *Ibid.*, 5: AAS 86 (1994), 236.

interpretation, Catholic exegetes must never forget that what they are interpreting is the *word of God*. Their common task is not finished when they have simply determined sources, defined forms or explained literary procedures. They arrive at the true goal of their work only when they have explained the meaning of the biblical text as God's word for today".[105]

The Council's biblical hermeneutic: a directive to be appropriated

34. Against this background, one can better appreciate the great principles of interpretation proper to Catholic exegesis set forth by the Second Vatican Council, especially in the Dogmatic Constitution *Dei Verbum*: "Seeing that, in sacred Scripture, God speaks through human beings in human fashion, it follows that the interpreters of sacred Scripture, if they are to ascertain what God has wished to communicate to us, should carefully search out the meaning which the sacred writers really had in mind, that meaning which God had thought well to manifest through the medium of their words".[106] On the one hand, the Council emphasizes the study of literary genres and historical context as basic elements for understanding the meaning intended

---

[105] PONTIFICAL BIBLICAL COMMISSION, *The Interpretation of the Bible in the Church* (15 April 1993), III, C, 1: *Enchiridion Vaticanum* 13, No. 3065.
[106] No. 12.

by the sacred author. On the other hand, since Scripture must be interpreted in the same Spirit in which it was written, the Dogmatic Constitution indicates three fundamental criteria for an appreciation of the divine dimension of the Bible: 1) the text must be interpreted with attention to *the unity of the whole of Scripture*; nowadays this is called canonical exegesis; 2) account is be taken of the *living Tradition of the whole Church*; and, finally, 3) respect must be shown for *the analogy of faith*. "Only where both methodological levels, the historical-critical and the theological, are respected, can one speak of a theological exegesis, an exegesis worthy of this book".[107]

The Synod Fathers rightly stated that the positive fruit yielded by the use of modern historical-critical research is undeniable. While today's academic exegesis, including that of Catholic scholars, is highly competent in the field of historical-critical methodology and its latest developments, it must be said that comparable attention need to be paid to the theological dimension of the biblical texts, so that they can be more deeply understood in accordance with the three elements indicated by the Dogmatic Constitution *Dei Verbum*.[108]

---

[107] BENEDICT XVI, *Intervention at the Fourteenth General Congregation of the Synod* (14 October 2008): *Insegnamenti* IV, 2 (2008), 493; cf. *Propositio* 25.

[108] Cf. *Propositio* 26.

35.   In this regard we should mention the serious risk nowadays of a dualistic approach to sacred Scripture. To distinguish two levels of approach to the Bible does not in any way mean to separate or oppose them, nor simply to juxtapose them. They exist only in reciprocity. Unfortunately, a sterile separation sometimes creates a barrier between exegesis and theology, and this "occurs even at the highest academic levels".[109] Here I would mention the most troubling consequences, which are to be avoided.

a) First and foremost, if the work of exegesis is restricted to the first level alone, Scripture ends up being *a text belonging only to the past*: "One can draw moral consequences from it, one can learn history, but the Book as such speaks only of the past, and exegesis is no longer truly theological, but becomes pure historiography, history of literature".[110] Clearly, such a reductive approach can never make it possible to comprehend the event of God's revelation through his word, which is handed down to us in the living Tradition and in Scripture.

b) The lack of a hermeneutic of faith with regard to Scripture entails more than a simple ab-

---

[109] *Propositio* 27.
[110] BENEDICT XVI, *Intervention at the Fourteenth General Congregation of the Synod* (14 October 2008): *Insegnamenti* IV, 2 (2008), 493; cf. *Propositio* 26.

sence; in its place there inevitably enters another hermeneutic, a positivistic and *secularized hermeneutic* ultimately based on the conviction that the Divine does not intervene in human history. According to this hermeneutic, whenever a divine element seems present, it has to be explained in some other way, reducing everything to the human element. This leads to interpretations that deny the historicity of the divine elements.[111]

c) Such a position can only prove harmful to the life of the Church, casting doubt over fundamental mysteries of Christianity and their historicity – as, for example, the institution of the Eucharist and the resurrection of Christ. A philosophical hermeneutic is thus imposed, one which denies the possibility that the Divine can enter and be present within history. The adoption of this hermeneutic within theological studies inevitably introduces a sharp dichotomy between an exegesis limited solely to the first level and a theology tending towards a spiritualization of the meaning of the Scriptures, one which would fail to respect the historical character of revelation.

All this is also bound to have a negative impact on the spiritual life and on pastoral activity; "as a consequence of the absence of the second methodological level, a profound gulf is opened up between scientific exegesis and *lectio divina*. This can give rise to a lack of clarity in the prepa-

[111] Cf. *ibid.*

ration of homilies".[112] It must also be said that this dichotomy can create confusion and a lack of stability in the intellectual formation of candidates for ecclesial ministries.[113] In a word, "where exegesis is not theology, Scripture cannot be the soul of theology, and conversely, where theology is not essentially the interpretation of the Church's Scripture, such a theology no longer has a foundation".[114] Hence we need to take a more careful look at the indications provided by the Dogmatic Constitution *Dei Verbum* in this regard.

Faith and reason in the approach to Scripture

36.   I believe that what Pope John Paul II wrote about this question in his Encyclical *Fides et Ratio* can lead to a fuller understanding of exegesis and its relationship to the whole of theology. He stated that we should not underestimate "the danger inherent in seeking to derive the truth of sacred Scripture from the use of one method alone, ignoring the need for a more comprehensive exegesis which enables the exegete, together with the whole Church, to arrive at the full sense of the texts. Those who devote themselves to the study of sacred Scripture should always remember that the various hermeneutical approaches have their

---

[112] *Ibid.*

[113] Cf. *Propositio* 27.

[114] BENEDICT XVI, *Intervention at the Fourteenth General Congregation of the Synod* (14 October 2008): *Insegnamenti* IV, 2 (2008), 493-494.

own philosophical underpinnings, which need to be carefully evaluated before they are applied to the sacred texts".[115]

This far-sighted reflection enables us to see how a hermeneutical approach to sacred Scripture inevitably brings into play the proper relationship between faith and reason. Indeed, the secularized hermeneutic of sacred Scripture is the product of reason's attempt structurally to exclude any possibility that God might enter into our lives and speak to us in human words. Here too, we need to urge a *broadening of the scope of reason*.[116] In applying methods of historical analysis, no criteria should be adopted which would rule out in advance God's self-disclosure in human history. The unity of the two levels at work in the interpretation of sacred Scripture presupposes, in a word, *the harmony of faith and reason*. On the one hand, it calls for a faith which, by maintaining a proper relationship with right reason, never degenerates into fideism, which in the case of Scripture would end up in fundamentalism. On the other hand, it calls for a reason which, in its investigation of the historical elements present in the Bible, is marked by openness and does not reject *a priori* anything beyond its own terms of reference. In any case, the religion of the incarnate *Logos* can hardly fail to appear profoundly reasonable to anyone who

---

[115] JOHN PAUL II, Encyclical Letter *Fides et Ratio* (14 September 1998), 55: AAS 91 (1999), 49-50.

[116] Cf. BENEDICT XVI, *Address to the Fourth National Ecclesial Congress in Italy* (19 October 2006): AAS 98 (2006), 804-815.

sincerely seeks the truth and the ultimate meaning of his or her own life and history.

Literal sense and spiritual sense

37.   A significant contribution to the recovery of an adequate scriptural hermeneutic, as the synodal assembly stated, can also come from renewed attention to the Fathers of the Church and their exegetical approach.[117] The Church Fathers present a theology that still has great value today because at its heart is the study of sacred Scripture as a whole. Indeed, the Fathers are primarily and essentially "commentators on sacred Scripture".[118] Their example can "teach modern exegetes a truly religious approach to sacred Scripture, and likewise an interpretation that is constantly attuned to the criterion of communion with the experience of the Church, which journeys through history under the guidance of the Holy Spirit".[119]

While obviously lacking the philological and historical resources at the disposal of modern exegesis, the patristic and mediaeval tradition could recognize the different senses of Scripture, beginning with the literal sense, namely, "the meaning conveyed by the words of Scripture and discovered by exegesis, following the rules of sound

---

[117]   Cf. *Propositio* 6.
[118]   Cf. SAINT AUGUSTINE, *De libero arbitrio*, III, XXI, 59: PL 32, 1300; *De Trinitate*, II, I, 2: PL 42, 845.
[119]   CONGREGATION FOR CATHOLIC EDUCATION, Instruction *Inspectis Dierum* (10 November 1989), 26: AAS 82 (1990), 618.

interpretation".[120] Saint Thomas of Aquinas, for example, states that "all the senses of sacred Scripture are based on the literal sense".[121] It is necessary, however, to remember that in patristic and medieval times every form of exegesis, including the literal form, was carried out on the basis of faith, without there necessarily being any distinction between the *literal sense* and the *spiritual sense*. One may mention in this regard the medieval couplet which expresses the relationship between the different senses of Scripture:

> "*Littera gesta docet, quid credas allegoria,*
> *Moralis quid agas, quo tendas anagogia.*
> The letter speaks of deeds; allegory about the faith;
> The moral about our actions; anagogy about our destiny".[122]

Here we can note the unity and interrelation between the *literal sense* and the *spiritual sense*, which for its part is subdivided into three senses which deal with the contents of the faith, with the moral life and with our eschatological aspiration.

In a word, while acknowledging the validity and necessity, as well as the limits, of the historical-critical method, we learn from the Fathers that exegesis "is truly faithful to the proper intention of biblical texts when it goes not only to the heart of their formulation to find the reality of

---

[120] *Catechism of the Catholic Church*, 116.
[121] *Summa Theologiae*, I, q. 1, art. 10, ad 1.
[122] *Catechism of the Catholic Church*, 118.

67

faith there expressed, but also seeks to link this reality to the experience of faith in our present world".[123] Only against this horizon can we recognize that the word of God is living and addressed to each of us in the here and now of our lives. In this sense, the Pontifical Biblical Commission's definition of the spiritual sense, as understood by Christian faith, remains fully valid: it is "the meaning expressed by the biblical texts when read, under the influence of the Holy Spirit, in the context of the paschal mystery of Christ and of the new life which flows from it. This context truly exists. In it the New Testament recognizes the fulfilment of the Scriptures. It is therefore quite acceptable to re-read the Scriptures in the light of this new context, which is that of life in the Spirit".[124]

The need to transcend the "letter"

38.   In rediscovering the interplay between the different senses of Scripture it thus becomes essential to grasp the *passage from letter to spirit*. This is not an automatic, spontaneous passage; rather, the letter needs to be transcended: "the word of God can never simply be equated with the letter of the text. To attain to it involves a progression and a process of understanding guided by the inner movement of the whole corpus, and hence it

---

[123] PONTIFICAL BIBLICAL COMMISSION, *The Interpretation of the Bible in the Church* (15 April 1993), II, A, 2: *Enchiridion Vaticanum* 13, No. 2987.
[124] *Ibid.*, II, B, 2: *Enchiridion Vaticanum* 13, No. 3003.

also has to become a vital process".[125] Here we see the reason why an authentic process of interpretation is never purely an intellectual process but also a lived one, demanding full engagement in the life of the Church, which is life "according to the Spirit" (*Gal* 5:16). The criteria set forth in Number 12 of the Dogmatic Constitution *Dei Verbum* thus become clearer: this progression cannot take place with regard to an individual literary fragment unless it is seen in relation to the whole of Scripture. Indeed, the goal to which we are necessarily progressing is the one Word. There is an inner drama in this process, since the passage that takes place in the power of the Spirit inevitably engages each person's freedom. Saint Paul lived this passage to the full in his own life. In his words: "*the letter kills, but the Spirit gives life*" (*2 Cor* 3:6), he expressed in radical terms the significance of this process of transcending the letter and coming to understand it only in terms of the whole. Paul discovered that "the Spirit of freedom has a name, and hence that freedom has an inner criterion: 'The Lord is the Spirit and where the Spirit of the Lord is, there is freedom' (*2 Cor* 3:17). The Spirit of freedom is not simply the exegete's own idea, the exegete's own vision. The Spirit is Christ, and Christ is the Lord who shows us the way".[126] We know that for Saint

[125] BENEDICT XVI, *Address to Representatives of the World of Culture at the "Collège des Bernardins" in Paris* (12 September 2008): AAS 100 (2008), 726.
[126] *Ibid.*

Augustine too this passage was at once dramatic and liberating; he came to believe the Scriptures – which at first sight struck him as so disjointed in themselves and in places so coarse – through the very process of transcending the letter which he learned from Saint Ambrose in typological interpretation, wherein the entire Old Testament is a path to Jesus Christ. For Saint Augustine, transcending the literal sense made the letter itself credible, and enabled him to find at last the answer to his deep inner restlessness and his thirst for truth.[127]

The Bible's intrinsic unity

39.   In the passage from letter to spirit, we also learn, within the Church's great tradition, to see the unity of all Scripture, grounded in the unity of God's word, which challenges our life and constantly calls us to conversion.[128] Here the words of Hugh of Saint Victor remain a sure guide: "All divine Scripture is one book, and this one book is Christ, speaks of Christ and finds its fulfilment in Christ".[129] Viewed in purely historical or literary terms, of course, the Bible is not a single book, but a collection of literary texts composed over the course of a thousand years or more, and its individual books are not easily seen to possess

---

[127] Cf. ID., *General Audience* (9 January 2008): *Insegnamenti* IV, 1 (2008), 41-45.

[128] Cf. *Propositio* 29.

[129] *De Arca Noe*, 2, 8: PL 176, 642C-D.

an interior unity; instead, we see clear inconsistencies between them. This was already the case with the Bible of Israel, which we Christians call the Old Testament. It is all the more so when, as Christians, we relate the New Testament and its writings as a kind of hermeneutical key to Israel's Bible, thus interpreting the latter as a path to Christ. The New Testament generally does not employ the term "Scripture" (cf. *Rom* 4:3; *1 Pet* 2:6), but rather "the Scriptures" (cf. *Mt* 21:43; *Jn* 5:39; *Rom* 1:2; *2 Pet* 3:16), which nonetheless are seen in their entirety as the one word of God addressed to us.[130] This makes it clear that the person of Christ gives unity to all the "Scriptures" in relation to the one "Word". In this way we can understand the words of Number 12 of the Dogmatic Constitution *Dei Verbum*, which point to the internal unity of the entire Bible as a decisive criterion for a correct hermeneutic of faith.

The relationship between the Old and the New Testaments

40.   Against this backdrop of the unity of the Scriptures in Christ, theologians and pastors alike need to be conscious of the relationship between Old and the New Testaments. First of all, it is evident that *the New Testament itself acknowledges the Old Testament as the word of God* and thus accepts the authority of the sacred Scriptures of the Jew-

---

[130]   Cf. BENEDICT XVI, *Address to Representatives of the World of Culture at the "Collège des Bernardins" in Paris* (12 September 2008): AAS 100 (2008), 725.

ish people.[131] It implicitly acknowledges them by using the same language and by frequently referring to passages from these Scriptures. It explicitly acknowledges them by citing many parts of them as a basis for argument. In the New Testament, an argument based on texts from the Old Testament thus has a definitive quality, superior to that of mere human argumentation. In the Fourth Gospel, Jesus states that "Scripture cannot be rejected" (*Jn* 10:35) and Saint Paul specifically makes clear that the Old Testament revelation remains valid for us Christians (cf. *Rom* 15:4; *1 Cor* 10:11).[132] We also affirm that "Jesus of Nazareth was a Jew and the Holy Land is the motherland of the Church":[133] the roots of Christianity are found in the Old Testament, and Christianity continually draws nourishment from these roots. Consequently, sound Christian doctrine has always resisted all new forms of Marcionism, which tend, in different ways, to set the Old Testament in opposition to the New.[134]

Moreover, the New Testament itself claims to be consistent with the Old and proclaims that in the mystery of the life, death and resurrec-

---

[131] Cf. *Propositio* 10; PONTIFICAL BIBLICAL COMMISSION, *The Jewish People and their Sacred Scriptures in the Christian Bible* (24 May 2001): *Enchiridion Vaticanum* 20, Nos. 748-755.

[132] Cf. *Catechism of the Catholic Church*, 121-122.

[133] *Propositio* 52.

[134] Cf. PONTIFICAL BIBLICAL COMMISSION, *The Jewish People and their Sacred Scriptures in the Christian Bible* (24 May 2001), 19: *Enchiridion Vaticanum* 20, Nos. 799-801; ORIGEN, *Homily on Numbers* 9, 4: SC 415, 238-242.

tion of Christ the sacred Scriptures of the Jewish people have found their perfect fulfilment. It must be observed, however, that the concept of the fulfilment of the Scriptures is a complex one, since it has three dimensions: a basic aspect of *continuity* with the Old Testament revelation, an aspect of *discontinuity* and an aspect of *fulfilment and transcendence*. The mystery of Christ stands in continuity of intent with the sacrificial cult of the Old Testament, but it came to pass in a very different way, corresponding to a number of prophetic statements and thus reaching a perfection never previously obtained. The Old Testament is itself replete with tensions between its institutional and its prophetic aspects. The paschal mystery of Christ is in complete conformity – albeit in a way that could not have been anticipated – with the prophecies and the foreshadowings of the Scriptures; yet it presents clear aspects of discontinuity with regard to the institutions of the Old Testament.

41.   These considerations show the unique importance of the Old Testament for Christians, while at the same time bringing out the *newness of Christological interpretation*. From apostolic times and in her living Tradition, the Church has stressed the unity of God's plan in the two Testaments through the use of typology; this procedure is in no way arbitrary, but is intrinsic to the events related in the sacred text and thus involves the whole of Scripture. Typology "discerns in God's works

of the Old Covenant prefigurations of what he accomplished in the fullness of time in the person of his incarnate Son".[135] Christians, then, read the Old Testament in the light of Christ crucified and risen. While typological interpretation manifests the inexhaustible content of the Old Testament from the standpoint of the New, we must not forget that the Old Testament retains its own inherent value as revelation, as our Lord himself reaffirmed (cf. *Mk* 12:29-31). Consequently, "the New Testament has to be read in the light of the Old. Early Christian catechesis made constant use of the Old Testament (cf. *1 Cor* 5:6-8; *1 Cor* 10:1-11)".[136] For this reason the Synod Fathers stated that "the Jewish understanding of the Bible can prove helpful to Christians for their own understanding and study of the Scriptures".[137]

"The New Testament is hidden in the Old and the Old is made manifest in the New",[138] as Saint Augustine perceptively noted. It is important, therefore, that in both pastoral and academic settings the close relationship between the two Testaments be clearly brought out, in keeping with the dictum of Saint Gregory the Great that "what the Old Testament promised, the New Testament made visible; what the former announces in a hidden way, the latter openly proclaims as present. Therefore the Old Testament is a prophecy of

---

[135] *Catechism of the Catholic Church*, 128.

[136] *Ibid.*, 129.

[137] *Propositio* 52.

[138] *Quaestiones in Heptateuchum*, 2, 73: PL 34, 623.

the New Testament; and the best commentary on the Old Testament is the New Testament".[139]

The "dark" passages of the Bible

42.   In discussing the relationship between the Old and the New Testaments, the Synod also considered those passages in the Bible which, due to the violence and immorality they occasionally contain, prove obscure and difficult. Here it must be remembered first and foremost that *biblical revelation is deeply rooted in history*. God's plan is manifested *progressively* and it is accomplished slowly, *in successive stages* and despite human resistance. God chose a people and patiently worked to guide and educate them. Revelation is suited to the cultural and moral level of distant times and thus describes facts and customs, such as cheating and trickery, and acts of violence and massacre, without explicitly denouncing the immorality of such things. This can be explained by the historical context, yet it can cause the modern reader to be taken aback, especially if he or she fails to take account of the many "dark" deeds carried out down the centuries, and also in our own day. In the Old Testament, the preaching of the prophets vigorously challenged every kind of injustice and violence, whether collective or individual, and thus became God's way of training his people in preparation for the Gospel. So it would be

---

[139]   *Homiliae in Ezechielem* I, VI, 15: PL 76, 836B.

a mistake to neglect those passages of Scripture that strike us as problematic. Rather, we should be aware that the correct interpretation of these passages requires a degree of expertise, acquired through a training that interprets the texts in their historical-literary context and within the Christian perspective which has as its ultimate hermeneutical key "the Gospel and the new commandment of Jesus Christ brought about in the paschal mystery".[140] I encourage scholars and pastors to help all the faithful to approach these passages through an interpretation which enables their meaning to emerge in the light of the mystery of Christ.

Christians, Jews and the sacred Scriptures

43. Having considered the close relationship between the New Testament and the Old, we now naturally turn to the special bond which that relationship has engendered between Christians and Jews, a bond that must never be overlooked. Pope John Paul II, speaking to Jews, called them "our 'beloved brothers' in the faith of Abraham, our Patriarch".[141] To acknowledge this fact is in no way to disregard the instances of discontinuity which the New Testament asserts with regard to the institutions of the Old Testament, much less the fulfilment of the Scriptures in the mystery of Jesus Christ, acknowledged as Messiah and Son

[140] *Propositio* 29.
[141] JOHN PAUL II, *Message to the Chief Rabbi of Rome* (22 May 2004): *Insegnamenti* XXVII, 1 (2004), p. 655.

of God. All the same, this profound and radical difference by no means implies mutual hostility. The example of Saint Paul (cf. *Rom* 9-11) shows on the contrary that "an attitude of respect, esteem and love for the Jewish people is the only truly Christian attitude in the present situation, which is a mysterious part of God's wholly positive plan".[142] Indeed, Saint Paul says of the Jews that: "as regards election they are beloved for the sake of their forefathers, for the gifts and the call of God are irrevocable!" (*Rom* 11:28-29).

Saint Paul also uses the lovely image of the olive tree to describe the very close relationship between Christians and Jews: the Church of the Gentiles is like a wild olive shoot, grafted onto the good olive tree that is the people of the Covenant (cf. *Rom* 11:17-24). In other words, we draw our nourishment from the same spiritual roots. We encounter one another as brothers and sisters who at certain moments in their history have had a tense relationship, but are now firmly committed to building bridges of lasting friendship.[143] As Pope John Paul II said on another occasion: "We have much in common. Together we can do much for peace, justice and for a more fraternal and more humane world".[144]

[142] Cf. PONTIFICAL BIBLICAL COMMISSION, *The Jewish People and their Sacred Scriptures in the Christian Bible* (24 May 2001), 87: *Enchiridion Vaticanum* 20, No. 1150.

[143] Cf. BENEDICT XVI, *Farewell Discourse at Ben Gurion International Airport in Tel Aviv* (15 May 2009): *Insegnamenti*, V, 1 (2009), 847-849.

[144] JOHN PAUL II, *Address to the Chief Rabbis of Israel* (23 March 2000): *Insegnamenti* XXIII, 1 (2000), 434.

I wish to state once more how much the Church values her *dialogue with the Jews*. Wherever it seems appropriate, it would be good to create opportunities for encounter and exchange in public as well as in private, and thus to promote growth in reciprocal knowledge, in mutual esteem and cooperation, also in the study of the sacred Scriptures.

The fundamentalist interpretation of sacred Scripture

44.   The attention we have been paying to different aspects of the theme of biblical hermeneutics now enables us to consider a subject which came up a number of times during the Synod: that of the fundamentalist interpretation of sacred Scripture.[145] The Pontifical Biblical Commission, in its document *The Interpretation of the Bible in the Church,* has laid down some important guidelines. Here I would like especially to deal with approaches which fail to respect the authenticity of the sacred text, but promote *subjective and arbitrary interpretations.* The "literalism" championed by the fundamentalist approach actually represents a betrayal of both the literal and the spiritual sense, and opens the way to various forms of manipulation, as, for example, by disseminating anti-ecclesial interpretations of the Scriptures. "The basic problem with fundamentalist interpretation is that, refusing to take into account the historical character

[145]   Cf. *Propositiones* 46 and 47.

of biblical revelation, it makes itself incapable of accepting the full truth of the incarnation itself. As regards relationships with God, fundamentalism seeks to escape any closeness of the divine and the human ... for this reason, it tends to treat the biblical text as if it had been dictated word for word by the Spirit. It fails to recognize that the word of God has been formulated in language and expression conditioned by various periods".[146] Christianity, on the other hand, perceives *in* the words *the* Word himself, the *Logos* who displays his mystery through this complexity and the reality of human history.[147] The true response to a fundamentalist approach is "the faith-filled interpretation of sacred Scripture". This manner of interpretation, "practised from antiquity within the Church's Tradition, seeks saving truth for the life of the individual Christian and for the Church. It recognizes the historical value of the biblical tradition. Precisely because of the tradition's value as an historical witness, this reading seeks to discover the living meaning of the sacred Scriptures for the lives of believers today",[148] while not ignoring the human mediation of the inspired text and its literary genres.

[146] PONTIFICAL BIBLICAL COMMISSION, *The Interpretation of the Bible in the Church* (15 April 1993), I, F: *Enchiridion Vaticanum* 13, No. 2974.

[147] Cf. BENEDICT XVI, *Address to Representatives of the World of Culture at the "Collège des Bernardins" in Paris* (12 September 2008): AAS 100 (2008), 726.

[148] *Propositio* 46.

45.   An authentic hermeneutic of faith has several important consequences for the Church's pastoral activity. The Synod Fathers themselves recommended, for example, a closer working relationship between pastors, exegetes and theologians. Episcopal Conferences might foster such encounters with the "aim of promoting greater communion in the service of the word of God".[149] Cooperation of this sort will help all to carry out their work more effectively for the benefit of the whole Church. For scholars too, this pastoral orientation involves approaching the sacred text with the realization that it is a message which the Lord addresses to us for our salvation. In the words of the Dogmatic Constitution *Dei Verbum*, "Catholic exegetes and other workers in the field of sacred theology should work diligently with one another and under the watchful eye of the sacred magisterium. Using appropriate techniques, they should together set about examining and explaining the sacred texts in such a way that as many as possible of those who are ministers of God's word may be able to dispense fruitfully the nourishment of the Scriptures to the people of God. This nourishment enlightens the mind, strengthens the will and fires the hearts of men and women with the love of God".[150]

[149] *Propositio* 28.
[150] SECOND VATICAN ECUMENICAL COUNCIL, Dogmatic Constitution on Divine Revelation *Dei Verbum*, 23.

46.   Conscious that the Church has her foundation in Christ, the incarnate Word of God, the Synod wished to emphasize the centrality of biblical studies within ecumenical dialogue aimed at the full expression of the unity of all believers in Christ.[151] The Scriptures themselves contain Jesus' moving prayer to the Father that his disciples might be one, so that the world may believe (cf. *Jn* 17:21). All this can only strengthen our conviction that by listening and meditating together on the Scriptures, we experience a real, albeit not yet full communion;[152] "shared listening to the Scriptures thus spurs us on towards the dialogue of charity and enables growth in the dialogue of truth".[153] Listening together to the word of God, engaging in biblical *lectio divina*, letting ourselves be struck by the inexhaustible freshness of God's word which never grows old, overcoming our deafness to those words that do not fit our own opinions or prejudices, listening and studying within the communion of the believers of every age: all these things represent a way of coming to unity in faith as a response to hearing the word of God.[154] The words of the Second Vatican Coun-

---

[151]   It should be recalled, however, that with regard to the so-called deuterocanonical books of the Old Testament and their inspiration, Catholics and Orthodox do not have exactly the same biblical canon as Anglicans and Protestants.

[152]   Cf. *Relatio post disceptationem*, 36.

[153]   *Propositio* 36.

[154]   Cf. BENEDICT XVI, *Address to the Eleventh Ordinary Council of the General Secretariat of the Synod of Bishops* (25 January 2007): AAS 99 (2007), 85-86.

cil were clear in this regard: "in [ecumenical] dialogue itself, sacred Scripture is a precious instrument in the mighty hand of God for attaining to that unity which the Saviour holds out to all".[155] Consequently, there should be an increase in ecumenical study, discussion and celebrations of the word of God, with due respect for existing norms and the variety of traditions.[156] These celebrations advance the cause of ecumenism and, when suitably carried out, they represent intense moments of authentic prayer asking God to hasten the day when we will all be able at last to sit at the one table and drink from the one cup. Nonetheless, while it is praiseworthy and right to promote such services, care must be taken that they are not proposed to the faithful as alternatives to the celebration of Holy Mass on Sundays or holydays of obligation.

In this work of study and prayer, we serenely acknowledge those aspects which still need to be explored more deeply and those on which we still differ, such as the understanding of the authoritative subject of interpretation in the Church and the decisive role of the magisterium.[157]

Finally, I wish to emphasize the statements of the Synod Fathers about the ecumenical im-

[155] SECOND VATICAN ECUMENICAL COUNCIL, Decree on Ecumenism *Unitatis Redintegratio*, 21.
[156] Cf. *Propositio* 36.
[157] Cf. SECOND VATICAN ECUMENICAL COUNCIL, Dogmatic Constitution on Divine Revelation *Dei Verbum*, 10.

portance of *translations of the Bible in the various languages*. We know that translating a text is no mere mechanical task, but belongs in some sense to the work of interpretation. In this regard, the Venerable John Paul II observed that "anyone who recalls how heavily debates about Scripture influenced divisions, especially in the West, can appreciate the significant step forward which these common translations represent".[158] Promoting common translations of the Bible is part of the ecumenical enterprise. I would like to thank all those engaged in this important work, and I encourage them to persevere in their efforts.

Consequences for the study of theology

47. A further consequence of an adequate hermeneutic of faith has to do with its necessary implications for exegetical and theological formation, particularly that of candidates for the priesthood. Care must be taken to ensure that the study of sacred Scripture is truly the soul of theology inasmuch as it is acknowledged as the word of God addressed to today's world, to the Church and to each of us personally. It is important that the criteria indicated in Number 12 of the Dogmatic Constitution *Dei Verbum* receive real attention and become the object of deeper study. A notion of scholarly research that would consider

[158] Encyclical Letter *Ut Unum Sint* (25 May 1995), 44: AAS 87 (1995), 947.

itself neutral with regard to Scripture should not be encouraged. As well as learning the original languages in which the Bible was written and suitable methods of interpretation, students need to have a deep spiritual life, in order to appreciate that the Scripture can only be understood if it is lived.

Along these lines, I urge that the study of the word of God, both handed down and written, be constantly carried out in a profoundly ecclesial spirit, and that academic formation take due account of the pertinent interventions of the magisterium, which "is not superior to the word of God, but is rather its servant. It teaches only what has been handed on to it. At the divine command and with the help of the Holy Spirit, it listens to this devoutly, guards it reverently and expounds it faithfully".[159] Care must thus be taken that the instruction imparted acknowledge that "sacred Tradition, sacred Scripture and the magisterium of the Church are so connected and associated that one of them cannot stand without the others".[160] It is my hope that, in fidelity to the teaching of the Second Vatican Council, the study of sacred Scripture, read within the communion of the universal Church, will truly be the soul of theological studies.[161]

---

[159] SECOND VATICAN ECUMENICAL COUNCIL, Dogmatic Constitution on Divine Revelation *Dei Verbum*, 10.

[160] *Ibid.*

[161] Cf. *ibid.,* 24.

The saints and the interpretation of Scripture

48.   The interpretation of sacred Scripture would remain incomplete were it not to include listening to *those who have truly lived the word of God: namely, the saints.*[162] Indeed, "*viva lectio est vita bonorum*".[163] The most profound interpretation of Scripture comes precisely from those who let themselves be shaped by the word of God through listening, reading and assiduous meditation.

It is certainly not by chance that the great currents of spirituality in the Church's history originated with an explicit reference to Scripture. I am thinking for example of Saint Anthony the Abbot, who was moved by hearing Christ's words: "if you would be perfect, go, sell what you possess and give to the poor, and you will have treasure in heaven; and come, follow me" (*Mt* 19:21).[164] No less striking is the question posed by Saint Basil the Great in the *Moralia*: "What is the distinctive mark of faith? Full and unhesitating certainty that the words inspired by God are true ... What is the distinctive mark of the faithful? Conforming their lives with the same complete certainty to the meaning of the words of Scripture, not daring to remove or add a single thing".[165] Saint Benedict, in his *Rule*, refers to Scripture as "a most perfect

---

[162] Cf. *Propositio* 22.
[163] Saint Gregory the Great, *Moralia in Job* XXIV, VIII, 16: PL 76, 295.
[164] Cf. Saint Athanasius, *Vita Antonii*, II: PL 73:127.
[165] *Moralia, Regula* LXXX, XXII: PG 31, 867.

norm for human life".[166] Saint Francis of Assisi –
we learn from Thomas of Celano – "upon hearing
that the disciples of Christ must possess neither
gold, nor silver nor money, nor carry a bag, nor
bread, nor a staff for the journey, nor sandals nor
two tunics ... exulting in the Holy Spirit, immediately cried out: 'This is what I want, this is what
I ask for, this I long to do with all my heart!'".[167]
Saint Clare of Assisi shared fully in the experience
of Saint Francis: "The form of life of the Order
of Poor Sisters – she writes – is this: to observe
the holy Gospel of our Lord Jesus Christ".[168] So
too, Saint Dominic "everywhere showed himself
to be a man of the Gospel, in word as in deed",[169]
and wanted his friars likewise to be "men of the
Gospel".[170] The Carmelite Saint Teresa of Avila,
who in her writings constantly uses biblical images to explain her mystical experiences, says that
Jesus himself revealed to her that "all the evil in
the world is derived from not knowing clearly the
truths of sacred Scripture".[171] Saint Thérèse of
the Child Jesus discovered that love was her personal vocation by poring over the Scriptures, es-

[166] *Rule*, 73, 3: SC 182, 672.
[167] THOMAS OF CELANO, *First Life of Saint Francis*, IX, 22:
FF 356.
[168] *Rule*, I, 1-2: FF 2750.
[169] BLESSED JORDAN OF SAXONY, *Libellus de principiis Ordinis Praedicatorum*, 104; *Monumenta Fratrum Praedicatorum Historica*,
Rome, 1935, 16, p. 75.
[170] ORDER OF FRIARS PREACHER, *First Constitutions* or *Con-
suetudines*, II, XXXI.
[171] *Vita*, 40, 1.

pecially Chapters 12 and 13 of the *First Letter to the Corinthians*;[172] the same saint describes the attraction of the Scriptures: "No sooner do I glance at the Gospel, but immediately I breathe in the fragrance of the life of Jesus and I know where to run".[173] Every saint is like a ray of light streaming forth from the word of God: we can think of Saint Ignatius of Loyola in his search for truth and in his discernment of spirits; Saint John Bosco in his passion for the education of the young; Saint John Mary Vianney in his awareness of the grandeur of the priesthood as gift and task; Saint Pius of Pietrelcina in his serving as an instrument of divine mercy; Saint Josemaria Escrivá in his preaching of the universal call to holiness; Blessed Teresa of Calcutta, the missionary of God's charity towards the poorest of the poor, and then the martyrs of Nazism and Communism, represented by Saint Teresa Benedicta of the Cross (Edith Stein), a Carmelite nun, and by Blessed Aloysius Stepinac, the Cardinal Archbishop of Zagreb.

49.   Holiness inspired by the word of God thus belongs in a way to the prophetic tradition, wherein the word of God sets the prophet's very life at its service. In this sense, holiness in the Church constitutes an interpretation of Scripture which cannot be overlooked. The Holy Spirit who inspired the sacred authors is the same Spirit who impels the saints to offer their lives for the Gos-

---

[172] Cf. *Story of a Soul*, Ms B, 254.
[173] *Ibid.*, Ms C, 35v.

pel. In striving to learn from their example, we set out on the sure way towards a living and effective hermeneutic of the word of God.

We saw a direct witness to this link between holiness and the word of God during the Twelfth Assembly of the Synod when four new saints were canonized on 12 October in Saint Peter's Square: Gaetano Errico, priest and founder of the Congregation of Missionaries of the Sacred Hearts of Jesus and Mary; Mother Maria Bernarda Bütler, a native of Switzerland and a missionary in Ecuador and Colombia; Sister Alphonsa of the Immaculate Conception, the first canonized saint born in India; and the young Ecuadorian laywoman Narcisa de Jesús Martillo Morán. With their lives they testified before the world and the Church to the perennial fruitfulness of Christ's Gospel. Through the intercession of these saints canonized at the time of the synodal assembly on the word of God, let us ask the Lord that our own lives may be that "good soil" in which the divine sower plants the word, so that it may bear within us fruits of holiness, "thirtyfold, sixtyfold, a hundredfold" (*Mk* 4:20).

PART TWO

VERBUM IN ECCLESIA

*"But to all who received him he gave power
to become children of God"
(Jn 1:12)*

The Church receives the word

50.   The Lord speaks his word so that it may be received by those who were created "through" that same word. "He came among his own" (*Jn* 1:11): his word is not something fundamentally alien to us, and creation was willed in a relationship of familiarity with God's own life. Yet the Prologue of the Fourth Gospel also places us before the rejection of God's word by "his own", who "received him not" (*Jn* 1:11). Not to receive him means not to listen to his voice, not to be conformed to the *Logos*. On the other hand, whenever men and women, albeit frail and sinful, are sincerely open to an encounter with Christ, a radical transformation begins to take place: "but to all who received him, he gave power to become children of God" (*Jn* 1:12). To receive the Word means to let oneself be shaped by him, and thus to be conformed by the power of the Holy Spirit to Christ, the "only Son from the Father" (*Jn* 1:14). It is the beginning of a new creation; a new creature is born, a new people comes to birth. Those who believe, that is to say, those who live the obedience of faith, are "born of God"

(*Jn* 1:13) and made sharers in the divine life: *sons in the Son* (cf. *Gal* 4:5-6; *Rom* 8:14-17). As Saint Augustine puts it nicely in commenting on this passage from John's Gospel: "you were created through the word, but now through the word you must be recreated".[174] Here we can glimpse the face of the Church as a reality defined by acceptance of the Word of God who, by taking flesh, came to pitch *his tent among us* (cf. *Jn* 1:14). This dwelling-place of God among men, this *shekinah* (cf. *Ex* 26:1), prefigured in the Old Testament, is now fulfilled in God's definitive presence among us in Christ.

Christ's constant presence in the life of the Church

51.   The relationship between Christ, the Word of the Father, and the Church cannot be fully understood in terms of a mere past event; rather, it is a living relationship which each member of the faithful is personally called to enter into. We are speaking of the presence of God's word to us today: "Lo, I am with you always, to the close of the age" (*Mt* 28:20). As Pope John Paul II has said: "Christ's relevance for people of all times is shown forth in his body, which is the Church. For this reason the Lord promised his disciples the Holy Spirit, who would 'bring to their remembrance' and teach them to understand his commandments (cf. *Jn* 14:26), and who would be the

---

[174] *In Iohannis Evangelium Tractatus*, I, 12: PL 35, 1385.

principle and constant source of a new life in the world (cf. *Jn* 3:5-8; *Rom* 8:1-13)".[175] The Dogmatic Constitution *Dei Verbum* expresses this mystery by using the biblical metaphor of a nuptial dialogue: "God, who spoke in the past, continues to converse with the spouse of his beloved Son. And the Holy Spirit, through whom the living voice of the Gospel rings out in the Church – and through it in the world – leads believers to the full truth and makes the word of Christ dwell in them in all its richness (cf. *Col* 3:16)."[176]

The Bride of Christ – the great teacher of the art of listening – today too repeats in faith: "Speak, Lord, your Church is listening".[177] For this reason the Dogmatic Constitution *Dei Verbum* intentionally begins with the words: "Hearing the word of God reverently and proclaiming it confidently, this sacred Council…".[178] Here we encounter a dynamic definition of the Church's life: "With these words the Council indicates a defining aspect of the Church: she is a community that hears and proclaims the word of God. The Church draws life not from herself but from the Gospel, and from the Gospel she discovers ever anew the direction for her journey. This is an approach that every Christian must understand and

[175] Encyclical Letter *Veritatis Splendor* (6 August 1993), 25: AAS 85 (1993), 1153.
[176] SECOND VATICAN ECUMENICAL COUNCIL, Dogmatic Constitution on Divine Revelation *Dei Verbum*, 8.
[177] *Relatio post disceptationem*, 11.
[178] No. 1.

apply to himself or herself: only those who first place themselves in an attitude of listening to the word can go on to become its heralds".[179] In the word of God proclaimed and heard, and in the sacraments, Jesus says today, here and now, to each person: "I am yours, I give myself to you"; so that we can receive and respond, saying in return: "I am yours".[180] The Church thus emerges as the milieu in which, by grace, we can experience what John tells us in the Prologue of his Gospel: "to all who received him he gave power to become children of God" (*Jn* 1:12).

THE LITURGY, PRIVILEGED SETTING
FOR THE WORD OF GOD

The word of God in the sacred liturgy

52.   In considering the Church as "*the home of the word*",[181] attention must first be given to the sacred liturgy, for the liturgy is the privileged setting in which God speaks to us in the midst of our lives; he speaks today to his people, who hear and respond. Every liturgical action is by its very nature steeped in sacred Scripture. In the words of the Constitution *Sacrosanctum Concilium*, "sacred Scripture is of the greatest importance in the

---

[179] BENEDICT XVI, *Address to the International Congress "Sacred Scripture in the Life of the Church"* (16 September 2005): AAS 97 (2005), 956.

[180] Cf. *Relatio post disceptationem,* 10.

[181] *Final Message,* III, 6.

celebration of the liturgy. From it are taken the readings, which are explained in the homily and the psalms that are sung. From Scripture the petitions, prayers and liturgical hymns receive their inspiration and substance. From Scripture the liturgical actions and signs draw their meaning".[182] Even more, it must be said that Christ himself "is present in his word, since it is he who speaks when Scripture is read in Church".[183] Indeed, "the liturgical celebration becomes the continuing, complete and effective presentation of God's word. The word of God, constantly proclaimed in the liturgy, is always a living and effective word through the power of the Holy Spirit. It expresses the Father's love that never fails in its effectiveness towards us".[184] The Church has always realized that in the liturgical action the word of God is accompanied by the interior working of the Holy Spirit who makes it effective in the hearts of the faithful. Thanks to the Paraclete, "the word of God becomes the foundation of the liturgical celebration, and the rule and support of all our life. The working of the same Holy Spirit ... brings home to each person individually everything that in the proclamation of the word of God is spoken for the good of the whole gathering. In strengthening the unity of all, the Holy

[182] SECOND VATICAN ECUMENICAL COUNCIL, Constitution on the Sacred Liturgy *Sacrosanctum Concilium*, 24.

[183] *Ibid.*, 7.

[184] *Ordo Lectionum Missae*, 4.

Spirit at the same time fosters a diversity of gifts and furthers their multiform operation".[185]

To understand the word of God, then, we need to appreciate and experience the essential meaning and value of the liturgical action. *A faith-filled understanding of sacred Scripture must always refer back to the liturgy*, in which the word of God is celebrated as a timely and living word: "In the liturgy the Church faithfully adheres to the way Christ himself read and explained the sacred Scriptures, beginning with his coming forth in the synagogue and urging all to search the Scriptures".[186]

Here one sees the sage pedagogy of the Church, which proclaims and listens to sacred Scripture following the rhythm of the liturgical year. This expansion of God's word in time takes place above all in the Eucharistic celebration and in the Liturgy of the Hours. At the centre of everything the paschal mystery shines forth, and around it radiate all the mysteries of Christ and the history of salvation which become sacramentally present: "By recalling in this way the mysteries of redemption, the Church opens up to the faithful the riches of the saving actions and the merits of her Lord, and makes them present to all times, allowing the faithful to enter into contact with them and to be filled with the grace of salvation".[187] For this reason I encourage the Church's

---

[185] *Ibid*, 9.

[186] *Ibid.*, 3; cf. *Lk* 4:16-21; 24:25-35, 44-49.

[187] SECOND VATICAN ECUMENICAL COUNCIL, Constitution on Sacred Liturgy *Sacrosanctum Concilium*, 102.

Pastors and all engaged in pastoral work to see that all the faithful learn to savour the deep meaning of the word of God which unfolds each year in the liturgy, revealing the fundamental mysteries of our faith. This is in turn the basis for a correct approach to sacred Scripture.

Sacred Scripture and the sacraments

53. In discussing the importance of the liturgy for understanding the word of God, the Synod of Bishops highlighted the relationship between sacred Scripture and the working of the sacraments. There is great need for a deeper investigation of the relationship between word and sacrament in the Church's pastoral activity and in theological reflection.[188] Certainly "the liturgy of the word is a decisive element in the celebration of each one of the sacraments of the Church";[189] in pastoral practice, however, the faithful are not always conscious of this connection, nor do they appreciate the unity between gesture and word. It is "the task of priests and deacons, above all when they administer the sacraments, to explain the unity between word and sacrament in the ministry of the Church".[190] The relationship between word

[188] Cf. BENEDICT XVI, Post-Synodal Apostolic Exhortation *Sacramentum Caritatis* (22 February 2007), 44-45: AAS 99 (2007) 139-141.

[189] PONTIFICAL BIBLICAL COMMISSION, *The Interpretation of the Bible in the Church* (15 April 1993) IV, C, 1: *Enchiridion Vaticanum* 13, No. 3123.

[190] *Ibid.*, III, B, 3: *Enchiridion Vaticanum* 13, No. 3056.

and sacramental gesture is the liturgical expression of God's activity in the history of salvation through the *performative character* of the word itself. In salvation history there is no separation between what God *says* and what he *does*. His word appears as alive and active (cf. *Heb* 4:12), as the Hebrew term *dabar* itself makes clear. In the liturgical action too, we encounter his word which accomplishes what it says. By educating the People of God to discover the performative character of God's word in the liturgy, we will help them to recognize his activity in salvation history and in their individual lives.

The word of God and the Eucharist

54.   What has been said in general about the relationship between the word and the sacraments takes on deeper meaning when we turn to the celebration of the Eucharist. The profound unity of word and Eucharist is grounded in the witness of Scripture (cf. *Jn* 6; *Lk* 24), attested to by the Fathers of the Church, and reaffirmed by the Second Vatican Council.[191] Here we think of Jesus'

---

[191]   Cf. SECOND VATICAN ECUMENICAL COUNCIL, Constitution on the Sacred Liturgy *Sacrosanctum Concilium*, 48, 51, 56; Dogmatic Constitution on Divine Revelation *Dei Verbum*, 21, 26; Decree on the Missionary Activity of the Church *Ad Gentes*, 6, 15; Decree on the Ministry and Life of Priests *Presbyterorum Ordinis*, 18; Decree on the Renewal of the Religious Life *Perfectae Caritatis*, 6. In the Church's great Tradition we find significant expressions such as "*Corpus Christi intelligitur etiam* [...] *Scriptura Dei*" ("God's Scripture is also understood as the Body of Christ"): WALTRAMUS, *De Unitate Ecclesiae Conservanda*, 1, 14, ed. W. Schwenkenbecher, Hanoverae, 1883, p. 33; "The flesh of the

discourse on the bread of life in the synagogue of Capernaum (cf. *Jn* 6:22-69), with its underlying comparison between Moses and Jesus, between the one who spoke face to face with God (cf. *Ex* 33:11) and the one who makes God known (cf. *Jn* 1:18). Jesus' discourse on the bread speaks of the gift of God, which Moses obtained for his people with the manna in the desert, which is really the *Torah*, the life-giving word of God (cf. *Ps* 119; *Pr* 9:5). In his own person Jesus brings to fulfilment the ancient image: "The bread of God is that which comes down from heaven and gives life to the world" … "I am the bread of life" (*Jn* 6:33-35). Here "the law has become a person. When we encounter Jesus, we feed on the living God himself, so to speak; we truly eat 'the bread from heaven'".[192] In the discourse at Capernaum, John's Prologue is brought to a deeper level. There God's *Logos* became flesh, but here this flesh becomes "*bread*" given for the life of the world (cf. *Jn* 6:51), with an allusion to Jesus' self-gift in the mystery of the cross, confirmed by the words about his blood being given as *drink* (cf. *Jn* 6:53). The mystery of the Eucharist reveals the true manna, the true bread of heaven: it is God's

Lord is true food and his blood true drink; this is the true good that is reserved for us in this present life, to nourish ourselves with his flesh and drink his blood, not only in the Eucharist but also in reading sacred Scripture. Indeed, true food and true drink is the word of God which we derive from the Scriptures": SAINT JEROME, *Commentarius in Ecclesiasten*, III: PL 23, 1092A.

[192] J. RATZINGER (BENEDICT XVI), *Jesus of Nazareth*, New York, 2007, 268.

Logos made flesh, who gave himself up for us in the paschal mystery.

Luke's account of the disciples on the way to Emmaus enables us to reflect further on this link between the hearing of the word and the breaking of the bread (cf. *Lk* 24:13-35). Jesus approached the disciples on the day after the Sabbath, listened as they spoke of their dashed hopes, and, joining them on their journey, "interpreted to them in all the Scriptures the things concerning himself" (24:27). The two disciples began to look at the Scriptures in a new way in the company of this traveller who seemed so surprisingly familiar with their lives. What had taken place in those days no longer appeared to them as failure, but as fulfilment and a new beginning. And yet, apparently not even these words were enough for the two disciples. The *Gospel of Luke* relates that "their eyes were opened and they recognized him" (24:31) only when Jesus took the bread, said the blessing, broke it and gave it to them, whereas earlier "their eyes were kept from recognizing him" (24:16). The presence of Jesus, first with his words and then with the act of breaking bread, made it possible for the disciples to recognize him. Now they were able to appreciate in a new way all that they had previously experienced with him: "Did not our hearts burn within us while he talked to us on the road, while he opened to us the Scriptures?" (24:32).

55.   From these accounts it is clear that Scripture itself points us towards an appreciation of

its own unbreakable bond with the Eucharist. "It can never be forgotten that the divine word, read and proclaimed by the Church, has as its one purpose the sacrifice of the new new covenant and the banquet of grace, that is, the Eucharist".[193] Word and Eucharist are so deeply bound together that we cannot understand one without the other: the word of God sacramentally takes flesh in the event of the Eucharist. The Eucharist opens us to an understanding of Scripture, just as Scripture for its part illumines and explains the mystery of the Eucharist. Unless we acknowledge the Lord's real presence in the Eucharist, our understanding of Scripture remains imperfect. For this reason "the Church has honoured the word of God and the Eucharistic mystery with the same reverence, although not with the same worship, and has always and everywhere insisted upon and sanctioned such honour. Moved by the example of her Founder, she has never ceased to celebrate his paschal mystery by coming together to read 'in all the Scriptures the things concerning him' (*Lk* 24:27) and to carry out the work of salvation through the celebration of the memorial of the Lord and through the sacraments".[194]

The sacramentality of the word

56.   Reflection on the performative character of the word of God in the sacramental action and a

---

[193] *Ordo Lectionum Missae*, 10.
[194] *Ibid.*

growing appreciation of the relationship between word and Eucharist lead to yet another significant theme which emerged during the synodal assembly, that of the *sacramentality* of the word.[195] Here it may help to recall that Pope John Paul II had made reference to the "*sacramental* character of revelation" and in particular to "the sign of the Eucharist in which the indissoluble unity between the signifier and signified makes it possible to grasp the depths of the mystery".[196] We come to see that at the heart of the sacramentality of the word of God is the mystery of the Incarnation itself: "the Word became flesh" (*Jn* 1:14), the reality of the revealed mystery is offered to us in the "flesh" of the Son. The Word of God can be perceived by faith through the "sign" of human words and actions. Faith acknowledges God's Word by accepting the words and actions by which he makes himself known to us. The sacramental character of revelation points in turn to the history of salvation, to the way that word of God enters time and space, and speaks to men and women, who are called to accept his gift in faith.

The sacramentality of the word can thus be understood by analogy with the real presence of Christ under the appearances of the consecrated bread and wine.[197] By approaching the altar and

---

[195] Cf. *Propositio* 7.

[196] Encyclical Letter *Fides et Ratio* (14 September 1998), 13: AAS 91 (1999), 16.

[197] Cf. *Catechism of the Catholic Church*, 1373-1374.

partaking in the Eucharistic banquet we truly share in the body and blood of Christ. The proclamation of God's word at the celebration entails an acknowledgment that Christ himself is present, that he speaks to us,[198] and that he wishes to be heard. Saint Jerome speaks of the way we ought to approach both the Eucharist and the word of God: "We are reading the sacred Scriptures. For me, the Gospel is the Body of Christ; for me, the holy Scriptures are his teaching. And when he says: *whoever does not eat my flesh and drink my blood* (*Jn* 6:53), even though these words can also be understood of the [Eucharistic] Mystery, Christ's body and blood are really the word of Scripture, God's teaching. When we approach the [Eucharistic] Mystery, if a crumb falls to the ground we are troubled. Yet when we are listening to the word of God, and God's Word and Christ's flesh and blood are being poured into our ears yet we pay no heed, what great peril should we not feel?".[199] Christ, truly present under the species of bread and wine, is analogously present in the word proclaimed in the liturgy. A deeper understanding of the sacramentality of God's word can thus lead us to a more unified understanding of the mystery of revelation, which takes place through "deeds and words intimately connected";[200] an apprecia-

---

[198] Cf. SECOND VATICAN ECUMENICAL COUNCIL, Constitution on Sacred Liturgy *Sacrosanctum Concilium*, 7.

[199] *In Psalmum* 147: CCL 78, 337-338.

[200] SECOND VATICAN ECUMENICAL COUNCIL, Dogmatic Constitution on Divine Revelation *Dei Verbum*, 2.

tion of this can only benefit the spiritual life of
the faithful and the Church's pastoral activity.

Sacred Scripture and the Lectionary

57.   In stressing the bond between word and
Eucharist, the Synod also rightly wanted to call attention to certain aspects of the celebration which
concern the service of the word. In the first place
I wish to mention the importance of the Lectionary. The reform called for by the Second Vatican
Council[201] has borne fruit in a richer access to sacred Scripture, which is now offered in abundance,
especially at Sunday Mass. The present structure
of the Lectionary not only presents the more important texts of Scripture with some frequency,
but also helps us to understand the unity of God's
plan thanks to the interplay of the Old and New
Testament readings, an interplay "in which Christ
is the central figure, commemorated in his paschal
mystery".[202] Any remaining difficulties in seeing
the relationship between those readings should be
approached in the light of canonical interpretation, that is to say, by referring to the inherent
unity of the Bible as a whole. Wherever necessary, the competent offices and groups can make
provision for publications aimed at bringing out
the interconnection of the Lectionary readings,
all of which are to be proclaimed to the liturgical

---

[201] Cf. Constitution on Sacred Liturgy *Sacrosanctum Concilium*, 107-108.
[202] *Ordo Lectionum Missae*, 66.

assembly as called for by the liturgy of the day. Other problems or difficulties should be brought to the attention of the Congregation for Divine Worship and the Discipline of the Sacraments.

Nor should we overlook the fact that the current Lectionary of the Latin rite has ecumenical significance, since it is used and valued also by communities not yet in full communion with the Catholic Church. The issue of the Lectionary presents itself differently in the liturgies of the Eastern Catholic Churches; the Synod requested that this issue be "examined authoritatively",[203] in accordance with the proper tradition and competences of the *sui iuris* Churches, likewise taking into account the ecumenical context.

Proclamation of the word and the ministry of Reader

58. The Synod on the Eucharist had already called for greater care to be taken in the proclamation of the word of God.[204] As is known, while the Gospel is proclaimed by a priest or deacon, in the Latin tradition the first and second readings are proclaimed by an appointed reader, whether a man or a woman. I would like to echo the Synod Fathers who once more stressed the need for the adequate training[205] of those who exercise the

[203] *Propositio* 16.
[204] BENEDICT XVI, Post-Synodal Apostolic Exhortation *Sacramentum Caritatis* (22 February 2007), 45: AAS 99 (2007), 140-141.
[205] Cf. *Propositio* 14.

munus of reader in liturgical celebrations,[206] and particularly those who exercise the ministry of Reader, which in the Latin rite is, as such, a lay ministry. All those entrusted with this office, even those not instituted in the ministry of Reader, should be truly suitable and carefully trained. This training should be biblical and liturgical, as well as technical: "The purpose of their biblical formation is to give readers the ability to understand the readings in context and to perceive by the light of faith central point of the revealed message. The liturgical formation ought to equip readers to have some grasp of the meaning and structure of the liturgy of the word and the significance of its connection with the liturgy of the Eucharist. The technical preparation should make the readers skilled in the art of reading publicly, either with the power of their own voice or with the help of sound equipment."[207]

The importance of the homily

59.   Each member of the People of God "has different duties and responsibilities with respect to the word of God. Accordingly, the faithful listen to God's word and meditate on it, but those who have the office of teaching by virtue of sacred ordination or have been entrusted with exercising that ministry", namely, bishops, priests and

---

[206] Cf. *Code of Canon Law*, cc. 230 §2; 204 §1.
[207] *Ordo Lectionum Missae*, 55

deacons, "expound the word of God".[208] Hence
we can understand the attention paid to the homily throughout the Synod. In the Apostolic Exhortation *Sacramentum Caritatis*, I pointed out
that "given the importance of the word of God,
the quality of homilies needs to be improved.
The homily 'is part of the liturgical action' and
is meant to foster a deeper understanding of
the word of God, so that it can bear fruit in the
lives of the faithful".[209] The homily is a means of
bringing the scriptural message to life in a way
that helps the faithful to realize that God's word
is present and at work in their everyday lives. It
should lead to an understanding of the mystery
being celebrated, serve as a summons to mission,
and prepare the assembly for the profession of
faith, the universal prayer and the Eucharistic liturgy. Consequently, those who have been charged
with preaching by virtue of a specific ministry
ought to take this task to heart. Generic and abstract homilies which obscure the directness of
God's word should be avoided, as well as useless
digressions which risk drawing greater attention
to the preacher than to the heart of the Gospel
message. The faithful should be able to perceive
clearly that the preacher has a compelling desire
to present Christ, who must stand at the centre
of every homily. For this reason preachers need
to be in close and constant contact with the sa-

[208] *Ibid.*, 8.
[209] No. 46: AAS 99 (2007), 141.

cred text;[210] they should prepare for the homily by meditation and prayer, so as to preach with conviction and passion. The synodal assembly asked that the following questions be kept in mind: "What are the Scriptures being proclaimed saying? What do they say to me personally? What should I say to the community in the light of its concrete situation?[211] The preacher "should be the first to hear the word of God which he proclaims",[212] since, as Saint Augustine says: "He is undoubtedly barren who preaches outwardly the word of God without hearing it inwardly".[213] The homily for Sundays and solemnities should be prepared carefully, without neglecting, whenever possible, to offer at weekday Masses *cum populo* brief and timely reflections which can help the faithful to welcome the word which was proclaimed and to let it bear fruit in their lives.

The fittingness of a Directory on Homiletics

60.   The art of good preaching based on the Lectionary is an art that needs to be cultivated. Therefore, in continuity with the desire expressed by the previous Synod,[214] I ask the competent

---

[210] Cf. SECOND VATICAN ECUMENICAL COUNCIL, Dogmatic Constitution on Divine Revelation *Dei Verbum*, 25.

[211] *Propositio* 15.

[212] *Ibid.*

[213] *Sermo* 179, 1: PL 38, 966.

[214] Cf. BENEDICT XVI, Post-Synodal Apostolic Exhortation *Sacramentum Caritatis* (22 February 2007), 93: AAS 99 (2007), 177.

authorities, along the lines of the Eucharistic Compendium,[215] also to prepare practical publications to assist ministers in carrying out their task as best they can: as for example a Directory on the homily, in which preachers can find useful assistance in preparing to exercise their ministry. As Saint Jerome reminds us, preaching needs to be accompanied by the witness of a good life: "Your actions should not contradict your words, lest when you preach in Church, someone may begin to think: 'So why don't you yourself act that way?' … In the priest of Christ, thought and word must be in agreement".[216]

The word of God, Reconciliation and the Anointing of the Sick

61.   Though the Eucharist certainly remains central to the relationship between God's word and the sacraments, we must also stress the importance of sacred Scripture in the other sacraments, especially the sacraments of healing, namely the sacrament of Reconciliation or Penance, and the sacrament of the Anointing of the Sick. The role of sacred Scripture in these sacraments is often overlooked, yet it needs to be assured its proper place. We ought never to forget that "the word of God is a word of reconciliation, for in it God has

[215] CONGREGATION FOR DIVINE WORSHIP AND THE DISCIPLINE OF THE SACRAMENTS, *Compendium Eucharisticum* (25 March 2009), Vatican City, 2009.
[216] *Epistula* 52, 7: CSEL 54, 426-427.

reconciled all things to himself (cf. *2 Cor* 5:18-20; *Eph* 1:10). The loving forgiveness of God, made flesh in Jesus, raises up the sinner".[217] "Through the word of God the Christian receives light to recognize his sins and is called to conversion and to confidence in God's mercy".[218] To have a deeper experience of the reconciling power of God's word, the individual penitent should be encouraged to prepare for confession by meditating on a suitable text of sacred Scripture and to begin confession by reading or listening to a biblical exhortation such as those provided in the rite. When expressing contrition it would be good if the penitent were to use "a prayer based on the words of Scripture",[219] such as those indicated in the rite. When possible, it would be good that at particular times of the year, or whenever the opportunity presents itself, individual confession by a number of penitents should take place within penitential celebrations as provided for by the ritual, with due respect for the different liturgical traditions; here greater time can be devoted to the celebration of the word through the use of suitable readings.

In the case of the sacrament of the Anointing of the Sick too, it must not be forgotten that "the healing power of the word of God is a constant call to the listener's personal conversion".[220]

[217] *Propositio* 8.
[218] *The Rite of Penance*, 17.
[219] *Ibid.*, 19.
[220] *Propositio* 8.

Sacred Scripture contains countless pages which speak of the consolation, support and healing which God brings. We can think particularly of Jesus' own closeness to those who suffer, and how he, God's incarnate Word, shouldered our pain and suffered out of love for us, thus giving meaning to sickness and death. It is good that in parishes and in hospitals, according to circumstances, community celebrations of the sacrament of the Anointing of the Sick should be held. On these occasions greater space should be given to the celebration of the word, and the sick helped to endure their sufferings in faith, in union with the redemptive sacrifice of Christ who delivers us from evil.

The word of God and the Liturgy of the Hours

62.   Among the forms of prayer which emphasize sacred Scripture, the Liturgy of the Hours has an undoubted place. The Synod Fathers called it "a privileged form of hearing the word of God, inasmuch as it brings the faithful into contact with Scripture and the living Tradition of the Church".[221] Above all, we should reflect on the profound theological and ecclesial dignity of this prayer. "In the Liturgy of the Hours, the Church, exercising the priestly office of her Head, offers 'incessantly' (*1 Th* 5:17) to God the sacrifice of praise, that is, the fruit of lips that confess his

[221] *Propositio* 19.

name (cf. *Heb* 13:15). This prayer is 'the voice of a bride speaking to her bridegroom, it is the very prayer that Christ himself, together with his Body, addressed to the Father'".[222] The Second Vatican Council stated in this regard that "all who take part in this prayer not only fulfil a duty of the Church, but also share in the high honour of the spouse of Christ; for by celebrating the praises of God, they stand before his throne in the name of the Church, their Mother".[223] The Liturgy of the Hours, as the public prayer of the Church, sets forth the Christian ideal of the sanctification of the entire day, marked by the rhythm of hearing the word of God and praying the Psalms; in this way every activity can find its point of reference in the praise offered to God.

Those who by virtue of their state in life are obliged to pray the Liturgy of the Hours should carry out this duty faithfully for the benefit of the whole Church. Bishops, priests and deacons aspiring to the priesthood, all of whom have been charged by the Church to celebrate this liturgy, are obliged to pray all the Hours daily.[224] As for the obligation of celebrating this liturgy in the Eastern Catholic Churches *sui iuris*, the prescriptions of their proper law are to be followed.[225] I also

---

[222] *Principles and Norms for the Liturgy of the Hours*, III, 15.
[223] Constitution on Sacred Liturgy *Sacrosanctum Concilium*, 85.
[224] Cf. *Code of Canon Law*, cc. 276 § 3, 1174 § 1.
[225] Cf. *Code of Canons of the Eastern Churches*, cc. 377; 473 § 1 and 2, 1°; 538 § 1; 881 § 1.

encourage communities of consecrated life to be exemplary in the celebration of the Liturgy of the Hours, and thus to become a point of reference and an inspiration for the spiritual and pastoral life of the whole Church.

The Synod asked that this prayer become more widespread among the People of God, particularly the recitation of Morning Prayer and Evening Prayer. This could only lead to greater familiarity with the word of God on the part of the faithful. Emphasis should also be placed on the value of the Liturgy of the Hours for the First Vespers of Sundays and Solemnities, particularly in the Eastern Catholic Churches. To this end I recommend that, wherever possible, parishes and religious communities promote this prayer with the participation of the lay faithful.

The word of God and the Book of Blessings

63.   Likewise, in using the Book of Blessings attention should be paid to the space allotted to proclaiming, hearing and briefly explaining the word of God. Indeed the act of blessing, in the cases provided for by the Church and requested by the faithful, should not be something isolated but related in its proper degree to the liturgical life of the People of God. In this sense a blessing, as a genuine sacred sign which "derives its meaning and effectiveness from God's word that

is proclaimed".[226] So it is important also to use these situations as means of reawakening in the faithful a hunger and thirst for every word that comes from the mouth of God (cf. *Mt* 4:4).

Suggestions and practical proposals for promoting fuller participation in the liturgy

64.   Having discussed some basic elements of the relationship between the liturgy and the word of God, I would now like to take up and develop several proposals and suggestions advanced by the Synod Fathers with a view to making the People of God ever more familiar with the word of God in the context of liturgical actions or, in any event, with reference to them.

a) *Celebrations of the word of God*

65.   The Synod Fathers encouraged all pastors to promote times devoted to the *celebration of the word* in the communities entrusted to their care.[227] These celebrations are privileged occasions for an encounter with the Lord. This practice will certainly benefit the faithful, and should be considered an important element of liturgical formation. Celebrations of this sort are particularly significant as a preparation for the Sunday Eucharist;

---

[226] *Book of Blessings*, Introduction, 21.
[227] Cf. *Propositio* 18; SECOND VATICAN ECUMENICAL COUNCIL, Constitution on Sacred the Liturgy *Sacrosanctum Concilium*, 35.

they are also a way to help the faithful to delve deeply into the riches of the Lectionary, and to pray and meditate on sacred Scripture, especially during the great liturgical seasons of Advent and Christmas, Lent and Easter. Celebrations of the word of God are to be highly recommended especially in those communities which, due to a shortage of clergy, are unable to celebrate the Eucharistic sacrifice on Sundays and holydays of obligation. Keeping in mind the indications already set forth in the Post-Synodal Apostolic Exhortation *Sacramentum Caritatis* with regard to Sunday celebrations in the absence of a priest,[228] I recommend that competent authorities prepare ritual directories, drawing on the experience of the particular Churches. This will favour, in such circumstances, celebrations of the word capable of nourishing the faith of believers, while avoiding the danger of the latter being confused with celebrations of the Eucharist: "on the contrary, they should be privileged moments of prayer for God to send holy priests after his own heart".[229]

The Synod Fathers also recommended celebrations of the word of God on pilgrimages, special feasts, popular missions, spiritual retreats and special days of penance, reparation or pardon. The various expressions of popular piety, albeit not liturgical acts and not to be confused

---

[228] Cf. BENEDICT XVI, Post-Synodal Apostolic Exhortation *Sacramentum Caritatis* (22 February 2007), 745: AAS 99 (2007), 162-163.
[229] *Ibid.*

with liturgical celebrations, should nonetheless be inspired by the latter and, above all, give due space to the proclamation and hearing of God's word; "popular piety can find in the word of God an inexhaustible source of inspiration, insuperable models of prayer and fruitful points for reflection".[230]

b) *The word and silence*

66.   In their interventions, a good number of Synod Fathers insisted on the importance of silence in relation to the word of God and its reception in the lives of the faithful.[231] The word, in fact, can only be spoken and heard in silence, outward and inward. Ours is not an age which fosters recollection; at times one has the impression that people are afraid of detaching themselves, even for a moment, from the mass media. For this reason, it is necessary nowadays that the People of God be educated in the value of silence. Rediscovering the centrality of God's word in the life of the Church also means rediscovering a sense of recollection and inner repose. The great patristic tradition teaches us that the mysteries of Christ all involve silence.[232] Only in silence can the

---

[230] CONGREGATION FOR DIVINE WORSHIP AND THE DISCIPLINE OF THE SACRAMENTS, *Directory of Popular Piety and the Liturgy, Principles and Guidelines* (17 December 2001), 87: *Enchiridion Vaticanum* 20, No. 2461.

[231] Cf. *Propositio* 14.

[232] Cf. SAINT IGNATIUS OF ANTIOCH, *Ad Ephesios*, XV, 2: *Patres Apostolici*, ed. F.X. FUNK, Tubingae, 1901, I, 224.

word of God find a home in us, as it did in Mary, woman of the word and, inseparably, woman of silence. Our liturgies must facilitate this attitude of authentic listening: *Verbo crescente, verba deficiunt*.[233]

The importance of all this is particularly evident in the Liturgy of the Word, "which should be celebrated in a way that favours meditation".[234] Silence, when called for, should be considered "a part of the celebration".[235] Hence I encourage Pastors to foster moments of recollection whereby, with the assistance of the Holy Spirit, the word of God can find a welcome in our hearts.

c) *The solemn proclamation of the word of God*

67. Another suggestion which emerged from the Synod was that the proclamation of the word of God, and the Gospel in particular, should be made more solemn, especially on major liturgical feasts, through the use of the Gospel Book, carried in procession during the opening rites and then brought to the lectern by a deacon or priest for proclamation. This would help the people of God to realize that "the reading of the Gospel is the high point of the liturgy of the word".[236] Following the indications contained in the *Ordo*

---

[233] SAINT AUGUSTINE, *Sermo* 288, 5: PL 38, 1307; *Sermo* 120, 2: PL 38, 677.

[234] *General Instruction of the Roman Missal*, 56

[235] *Ibid.*, 45; cf. SECOND VATICAN ECUMENICAL COUNCIL, Constitution on Sacred Liturgy *Sacrosanctum Concilium*, 30.

[236] *Ordo Lectionum Missae*, 13.

Lectionum Missae, it is good that the word of God, especially the Gospel, be enhanced by being proclaimed in song, particularly on certain solemnities. The greeting, the initial announcement: "A reading from the holy Gospel" and the concluding words: "The Gospel of the Lord", could well be sung as a way of emphasizing the importance of what was read.[237]

d) *The word of God in Christian churches*

68.   In order to facilitate hearing the word of God, consideration should be given to measures which can help focus the attention of the faithful. Concern should be shown for church acoustics, with due respect for liturgical and architectural norms. "Bishops, duly assisted, in the construction of churches should take care that they be adapted to the proclamation of the word, to meditation and to the celebration of the Eucharist. Sacred spaces, even apart from the liturgical action, should be eloquent and should present the Christian mystery in relation to the word of God".[238]

Special attention should be given to the *ambo* as the liturgical space from which the word of God is proclaimed. It should be located in a clearly visible place to which the attention of the faithful will be naturally drawn during the liturgy of the word. It should be fixed, and decorated in aes-

---

[237]   Cf. *ibid.*, 17.
[238]   *Propositio* 40.

thetic harmony with the *altar*, in order to present visibly the theological significance of *the double table of the word and of the Eucharist*. The readings, the responsorial psalm and the Exsultet are to be proclaimed from the ambo; it can also be used for the homily and the prayers of the faithful.[239]

The Synod Fathers also proposed that churches give a place of honour to the sacred Scriptures, even *outside of liturgical celebrations*.[240] It is good that the book which contains the word of God should enjoy a visible place of honour inside the Christian temple, without prejudice to the central place proper to the tabernacle containing the Blessed Sacrament.[241]

e) *The exclusive use of biblical texts in the liturgy*

69.   The Synod also clearly reaffirmed a point already laid down by liturgical law,[242] namely that *the readings drawn from sacred Scripture may never be replaced by other texts*, however significant the latter may be from a spiritual or pastoral standpoint: "No text of spirituality or literature can equal the value and riches contained in sacred Scripture, which is the word of God".[243] This is an ancient rule of the Church which is to be maintained.[244]

---

[239] Cf . *General Instruction of the Roman Missal*, 309.

[240] Cf. *Propositio* 14.

[241] BENEDICT XVI, Post-Synodal Apostolic Exhortation *Sacramentum Caritatis* (22 February 2007), 69: AAS 99 (2007), 157.

[242] Cf. *General Instruction of the Roman Missal*, 57.

[243] *Propositio* 14.

[244] Cf. Canon 36 of the *Synod of Hippo*, in the year 399: DS 186.

In the face of certain abuses, Pope John Paul II had already reiterated the importance of never using other readings in place of sacred Scripture.[245] It should also be kept in mind that the *Responsorial Psalm* is also the word of God, and hence should not be replaced by other texts; indeed it is most appropriate that it be sung.

f) *Biblically-inspired liturgical song*

70.   As part of the enhancement of the word of God in the liturgy, attention should also be paid to the use of song at the times called for by the particular rite. Preference should be given to songs which are of clear biblical inspiration and which express, through the harmony of music and words, the beauty of God's word. We would do well to make the most of those songs handed down to us by the Church's tradition which respect this criterion. I think in particular of the importance of Gregorian chant.[246]

g) *Particular concern for the visually and hearing impaired*

71.   Here I wish also to recall the Synod's recommendation that special attention be given to those

---

[245] Cf. JOHN PAUL II, Apostolic Letter *Vicesimus Quintus Annus* (4 December 1988), 13: AAS 81 (1989) 910; CONGREGATION FOR DIVINE WORSHIP AND THE DISCIPLINE OF THE SACRAMENTS, Instruction *Redemptionis Sacramentum* (25 March 2004), 62: *Enchiridion Vaticanum* 22, No. 2248.

[246] Cf. SECOND VATICAN ECUMENICAL COUNCIL, Constitution on Sacred Liturgy *Sacrosanctum Concilium*, 116; *General Instruction of the Roman Missal*, 41.

who encounter problems in participating actively in the liturgy; I think, for example, of the visually and hearing impaired. I encourage our Christian communities to offer every possible practical assistance to our brothers and sisters suffering from such impairments, so that they too can be able to experience a living contact with the word of the Lord.[247]

THE WORD OF GOD IN THE LIFE OF THE CHURCH

Encountering the word of God in sacred Scripture

72.   If it is true that the liturgy is the privileged place for the proclamation, hearing and celebration of the word of God, it is likewise the case that this encounter must be prepared in the hearts of the faithful and then deepened and assimilated, above all by them. The Christian life is essentially marked by an encounter with Jesus Christ, who calls us to follow him. For this reason, the Synod of Bishops frequently spoke of the importance of pastoral care in the Christian communities as the proper setting where a personal and communal journey based on the word of God can occur and truly serve as the basis for our spiritual life. With the Synod Fathers I express my heartfelt hope for the flowering of "a new season of greater love for sacred Scripture on the part of every member of the People of God, so that their

<hr>

[247] Cf. *Propositio* 14.

prayerful and faith-filled reading of the Bible will, with time, deepen their personal relationship with Jesus".[248]

Throughout the history of the Church, numerous saints have spoken of the need for knowledge of Scripture in order to grow in love for Christ. This is evident particularly in the Fathers of the Church. Saint Jerome, in his great love for the word of God, often wondered: "How could one live without the knowledge of Scripture, by which we come to know Christ himself, who is the life of believers?".[249] He knew well that the Bible is the means "by which God speaks daily to believers".[250] His advice to the Roman matron Leta about raising her daughter was this: "Be sure that she studies a passage of Scripture each day... Prayer should follow reading, and reading follow prayer... so that in the place of jewellery and silk, she may love the divine books".[251] Jerome's counsel to the priest Nepotian can also be applied to us: "Read the divine Scriptures frequently; indeed, the sacred book should never be out of your hands. Learn there what you must teach".[252] Let us follow the example of this great saint who devoted his life to the study of the Bible and who gave the Church its Latin translation, the Vulgate, as well as the example of all those saints who

---

[248] *Propositio* 9.
[249] *Epistula* 30, 7: CSEL 54, p. 246.
[250] ID., *Epistula* 133, 13: CSEL 56, p. 260.
[251] ID., *Epistula* 107, 9, 12: CSEL 55, pp. 300, 302.
[252] ID., *Epistula* 52, 7: CSEL 54, p. 426.

made an encounter with Christ the centre of their spiritual lives. Let us renew our efforts to understand deeply the word which God has given to his Church: thus we can aim for that "high standard of ordinary Christian living"[253] proposed by Pope John Paul II at the beginning of the third Christian millennium, which finds constant nourishment in attentively hearing the word of God.

Letting the Bible inspire pastoral activity

73.   Along these lines the Synod called for a particular pastoral commitment to emphasizing the centrality of the word of God in the Church's life, and recommended a greater "biblical apostolate", not alongside other forms of pastoral work, but as *a means of letting the Bible inspire all pastoral work*".[254] This does not mean adding a meeting here or there in parishes or dioceses, but rather of examining the ordinary activities of Christian communities, in parishes, associations and movements, to see if they are truly concerned with fostering a personal encounter with Christ, who gives himself to us in his word. Since "ignorance of the Scriptures is ignorance of Christ",[255] making the Bible the inspiration of every ordinary and extraordinary

---

[253] JOHN PAUL II, Apostolic Letter *Novo Millennio Ineunte* (6 January 2001), 31: AAS 93 (2001), 287-288.

[254] *Propositio* 30; cf. SECOND VATICAN ECUMENICAL COUNCIL, Dogmatic Constitution on Divine Revelation *Dei Verbum*, 24.

[255] SAINT JEROME, *Commentariorum in Isaiam libri*, *Prol.*: PL 24, 17B.

pastoral outreach will lead to a greater awareness of the person of Christ, who reveals the Father and is the fullness of divine revelation.

For this reason I encourage pastors and the faithful to recognize the importance of this emphasis on the Bible: it will also be the best way to deal with certain pastoral problems which were discussed at the Synod and have to do, for example, with the *proliferation of sects* which spread a distorted and manipulative reading of sacred Scripture. Where the faithful are not helped to know the Bible in accordance with the Church's faith and based on her living Tradition, this pastoral vacuum becomes fertile ground for realities like the sects to take root. Provision must also be made for the suitable preparation of priests and lay persons who can instruct the People of God in the genuine approach to Scripture.

Furthermore, as was brought out during the Synod sessions, it is good that pastoral activity also favour the growth of *small communities*, "formed by families or based in parishes or linked to the different ecclesial movements and new communities",[256] which can help to promote formation, prayer and knowledge of the Bible in accordance with the Church's faith.

The biblical dimension of catechesis

74.   An important aspect of the Church's pastoral work which, if used wisely, can help in re-

[256] *Propositio* 21.

discovering the centrality of God's word is catechesis, which in its various forms and levels must
constantly accompany the journey of the People
of God. Luke's description (cf. *Lk* 24:13-35) of
the disciples who meet Jesus on the road to Emmaus represents, in some sense, the model of a
catechesis centred on "the explanation of the
Scriptures", an explanation which Christ alone
can give (cf. *Lk* 24:27-28), as he shows that they
are fulfilled in his person.[257] The hope which tri-
umphs over every failure was thus reborn, and
made those disciples convinced and credible witnesses of the Risen Lord.

The *General Catechetical Directory* contains valuable guidelines for a biblically inspired catche-
sis and I readily encourage that these be consult-
ed.[258] Here I wish first and foremost to stress that
catechesis "must be permeated by the mindset,
the spirit and the outlook of the Bible and the
Gospels through assiduous contact with the texts
themselves; yet it also means remembering that
catechesis will be all the richer and more effective for reading the texts with the mind and the
heart of the Church",[259] and for drawing inspiration from the two millennia of the Church's re-

---

[257] Cf. *Propositio* 23.
[258] Cf. CONGREGATION FOR THE CLERGY, *General Catechetical Directory* (15 August 1997), 94-96; *Enchiridion Vaticanum*, 16,
Nos. 875-878; JOHN PAUL II, Apostolic Exhortation *Catechesi
Tradendae* (16 October 1979), 27: AAS 71 (1979), 1298-1299.
[259] *Ibid.*, 127: *Enchiridion Vaticanum* 16, No. 935; cf. JOHN
PAUL II, Apostolic Exhortation *Catechesi Tradendae* (16 October
1979), 27: AAS 71 (1979), 1299.

flection and life. A knowledge of biblical person-
ages, events and well-known sayings should thus
be encouraged; this can also be promoted by the
judicious *memorization* of some passages which are
particularly expressive of the Christian mysteries. Catechetical work always entails approaching
Scripture in faith and in the Church's Tradition,
so that its words can be perceived as living, just
as Christ is alive today wherever two or three are
gathered in his name (cf. *Mt* 18:20). Catechesis
should communicate in a lively way the history of
salvation and the content of the Church's faith,
and so enable every member of the faithful to
realize that this history is also a part of his or her
own life.

Here it is important to stress the relationship
between sacred Scripture and the *Catechism of the
Catholic Church*, as it is set forth in the *General Catechetical Directory*: "Sacred Scripture, in fact, as 'the
word of God written under the inspiration of the
Holy Spirit', and the Catechism of the Catholic
Church, as a significant contemporary expression
of the living Tradition of the Church and a sure
norm for teaching the faith, are called, each in its
own way and according to its specific authority, to
nourish catechesis in the Church today".[260]

The biblical formation of Christians

75.   In order to achieve the goal set by the Synod, namely, an increased emphasis on the Bible in

---

[260] *Ibid.*, 128: *Enchiridion Vaticanum* 16, No. 936.

the Church's pastoral activity, all Christians, and catechists in particular, need to receive suitable training. Attention needs to be paid to the *biblical apostolate*, which is a very valuable means to that end, as the Church's experience has shown. The Synod Fathers also recommended that, possibly through the use of existing academic structures, centres of formation should be established where laity and missionaries can be trained to understand, live and proclaim the word of God. Also, where needed, specialized institutes for biblical studies should be established to ensure that exegetes possess a solid understanding of theology and an appropriate appreciation for the contexts in which they carry out their mission.[261]

Sacred Scripture in large ecclesial gatherings

76.   Among a variety of possible initiatives, the Synod suggested that in meetings, whether at the diocesan, national or international levels, greater emphasis be given to the importance of the word of God, its attentive hearing, and the faith-filled and prayerful reading of the Bible. In Eucharistic Congresses, whether national or international, at World Youth Days and other gatherings, it would be praiseworthy to make greater room for the celebration of the word and for biblically-inspired moments of formation.[262]

---

[261] Cf. *Propositio* 33.
[262] Cf. *Propositio* 45.

77.   In stressing faith's intrinsic summons to an ever deeper relationship with Christ, the word of God in our midst, the Synod also emphasized that this word calls each one of us personally, revealing that *life itself is a vocation* from God. In other words, the more we grow in our personal relationship with the Lord Jesus, the more we realize that he is calling us to holiness in and through the definitive choices by which we respond to his love in our lives, taking up tasks and ministries which help to build up the Church. This is why the Synod frequently encouraged all Christians to grow in their relationship with the word of God, not only because of their Baptism, but also in accordance with their call to various states in life. Here we touch upon one of the pivotal points in the teaching of the Second Vatican Council, which insisted that each member of the faithful is called to holiness according to his or her proper state in life.[263] Our call to holiness is revealed in sacred Scripture: "Be holy, for I am holy" (*Lev* 11:44; 19:2; 20:7). Saint Paul then points out its Christological basis: in Christ, the Father "has chosen us before the foundation of the world, that we should be holy and blameless before him" (*Eph* 1:4). Paul's greeting to his brothers and sisters in the community of Rome can be taken as addressed to each of us: "To all God's beloved, who are called to be saints:

---

[263] Cf. SECOND VATICAN ECUMENICAL COUNCIL, Dogmatic Constitution on the Church *Lumen Gentium*, 39-42.

grace to you and peace from God our Father and the Lord Jesus Christ!" (*Rom* 1:7).

a) *Ordained ministers and the word of God*

78.   I would like to speak first to the Church's ordained ministers, in order to remind them of the Synod's statement that "the word of God is indispensable in forming the heart of a good shepherd and minister of the word".[264] Bishops, priests, and deacons can hardly think that they are living out their vocation and mission apart from a decisive and renewed commitment to sanctification, one of whose pillars is contact with God's word.

79.   To those called to the *episcopate*, who are the first and most authoritative heralds of the word, I would repeat the words of Pope John Paul II in his Post-Synodal Apostolic Exhortation *Pastores Gregis*. For the nourishment and progress of his spiritual life, the Bishop must always put "in first place, reading and meditation on the word of God. Every Bishop must commend himself and feel himself commended 'to the Lord and to the word of his grace, which is able to build up and to give the inheritance among all those who are sanctified' (*Acts* 20:32). Before becoming one who hands on the word, the Bishop, together with his priests and indeed like every member of the faithful, and like the Church herself, must be

[264] *Propositio* 31.

a hearer of the word. He should dwell 'within' the word and allow himself to be protected and nourished by it, as if by a mother's womb".[265] To all my brother Bishops I recommend frequent personal reading and study of sacred Scripture, in imitation of Mary, *Virgo Audiens* and Queen of the Apostles.

80. To *priests* too, I would recall the words of Pope John Paul II, who in the Post-Synodal Apostolic Exhortation *Pastores Dabo Vobis*, stated that "the priest is first of all a *minister of the word of God*, consecrated and sent to announce the Good News of the Kingdom to all, calling every person to the obedience of faith and leading believers to an ever increasing knowledge of and communion in the mystery of God, as revealed and communicated to us in Christ. For this reason the priest himself ought first of all to develop a great personal familiarity with the word of God. Knowledge of its linguistic and exegetical aspects, though certainly necessary, is not enough. He needs to approach the word with a docile and prayerful heart so that it may deeply penetrate his thoughts and feelings and bring about a new outlook in him – 'the mind of Christ' (*1 Cor* 2:16)".[266] Consequently, his words, his choices and his behaviour must increasingly become a reflection, proclamation and witness of the Gospel; "only

[265] No. 15: AAS 96 (2004), 846-847.
[266] No. 26: AAS 84 (1992), 698.

if he 'abides' in the word will the priest become a perfect disciple of the Lord. Only then then will he know the truth and be set truly free".[267]

In a word, the priestly vocation demands that one be *consecrated "in the truth"*. Jesus states this clearly with regard to his disciples: "Sanctify them in the truth; your word is truth. As you have sent me into the world, so I have sent them into the world" (*Jn* 17:17-18). The disciples in a certain sense become "drawn into intimacy with God by being immersed in the word of God. God's word is, so to speak, the purifying bath, the creative power which changes them and makes them belong to God".[268] And since Christ himself is God's Word made flesh (*Jn* 1:14) – "the Truth" (*Jn* 14:6) – Jesus' prayer to the Father, "Sanctify them in the truth", means in the deepest sense: "Make them one with me, the Christ. Bind them to me. Draw them into me. For there is only one priest of the New Covenant, Jesus Christ himself".[269] Priests need to grow constantly in their awareness of this reality.

81.   I would also like to speak of the place of God's word in the life of those called to the *diaconate*, not only as the final step towards the order of priesthood, but as a permanent service. The *Directory for the Permanent Diaconate* states that "the

---

[267] *Ibid.*

[268] BENEDICT XVI, *Homily at the Chrism Mass* (9 April 2009): AAS 101 (2009), 355.

[269] *Ibid.*, 356.

deacon's theological identity clearly provides the features of his specific spirituality, which is presented essentially as a spirituality of service. The model *par excellence* is Christ as servant, lived totally at the service of God, for the good of humanity".[270] From this perspective, one can see how, in the various dimensions of the diaconal ministry, a "characteristic element of diaconal spirituality is the word of God, of which the deacon is called to be an authoritative preacher, believing what he preaches, teaching what he believes, and living what he teaches".[271] Hence, I recommend that deacons nourish their lives by the faith-filled reading of sacred Scripture, accompanied by study and prayer. They should be introduced to "sacred Scripture and its correct interpretation; to the relationship between Scripture and Tradition; in particular to the use of Scripture in preaching, in catechesis and in pastoral activity in general".[272]

b) *The word of God and candidates for Holy Orders*

82. The Synod attributed particular importance to the decisive role that the word of God must play in the spiritual life of candidates for the ministerial priesthood: "Candidates for the priesthood must learn to love the word of God. Scrip-

---

[270] CONGREGATION FOR CATHOLIC EDUCATION, *Fundamental Norms for the Formation of Permanent Deacons* (22 February 1998), 11: *Enchiridion Vaticanum* 17, Nos. 174-175.

[271] *Ibid.*, 74: *Enchiridion Vaticanum* 17, No. 263.

[272] *Ibid.*, 81: *Enchiridion Vaticanum* 17, No. 271.

ture should thus be the soul of their theological formation, and emphasis must be given to the indispensable interplay of exegesis, theology, spirituality and mission".[273] Those aspiring to the ministerial priesthood are called to a profound personal relationship with God's word, particularly in *lectio divina*, so that this relationship will in turn nurture their vocation: it is in the light and strength of God's word that one's specific vocation can be discerned and appreciated, loved and followed, and one's proper mission carried out, by nourishing the heart with thoughts of God, so that faith, as our response to the word, may become a new criterion for judging and evaluating persons and things, events and issues.[274]

Such attention to the prayerful reading of Scripture must not in any way lead to a dichotomy with regard to the exegetical studies which are a part of formation. The Synod recommended that seminarians be concretely helped to see *the relationship between biblical studies and scriptural prayer.* The study of Scripture ought to lead to an increased awareness of the mystery of divine revelation and foster an attitude of prayerful response to the Lord who speaks. Conversely, an authentic life of prayer cannot fail to nurture in the candidate's heart a desire for greater knowledge of the God who has revealed himself in his word as

[273] *Propositio* 32.
[274] Cf. JOHN PAUL II, Post-Synodal Apostolic Exhortation *Pastores Dabo Vobis* (25 March 1992), 47: AAS 84 (1992), 740-742.

infinite love. Hence, great care should be taken to ensure that seminarians always cultivate this *reciprocity between study and prayer* in their lives. This end will be served if candidates are introduced to the study of Scripture through methods which favour this integral approach.

c) *The word of God and the consecrated life*

83. With regard to the consecrated life, the Synod first recalled that it "is born from hearing the word of God and embracing the Gospel as its rule of life".[275] A life devoted to following Christ in his chastity, poverty and obedience thus becomes "a living 'exegesis' of God's word".[276] The Holy Spirit, in whom the Bible was written, is the same Spirit who illumines "the word of God with new light for the founders and foundresses. Every charism and every rule springs from it and seeks to be an expression of it",[277] thus opening up new pathways of Christian living marked by the radicalism of the Gospel.

Here I would mention that the great monastic tradition has always considered meditation on

[275] *Propositio* 24.

[276] BENEDICT XVI, *Homily for the World Day of Consecrated Life* (2 February 2008): AAS 100 (2008), 133; cf. JOHN PAUL II, Post-Synodal Apostolic Exhortation *Vita Consecrata* (25 March 1996), 82: AAS 88 (1996), 458-460.

[277] CONGREGATION FOR INSTITUTES OF CONSECRATED LIFE AND FOR SOCIETIES OF APOSTOLIC LIFE, Instruction *Starting Afresh from Christ: A Renewed Commitment to Consecrated Life in the Third Millennium* (19 May 2002), 24: *Enchiridion Vaticanum* 21, No. 447.

sacred Scripture to be an essential part of its specific spirituality, particularly in the form of *lectio divina*. Today too, both old and new expressions of special consecration are called to be genuine schools of the spiritual life, where the Scriptures can be read according to the Holy Spirit in the Church, for the benefit of the entire People of God. The Synod therefore recommended that communities of consecrated life always make provision for solid instruction in the faith-filled reading of the Bible.[278]

Once again I would like to echo the consideration and gratitude that the Synod expressed with regard to those forms of *contemplative life* whose specific charism is to devote a great part of their day to imitating the Mother of God, who diligently pondered the words and deeds of her Son (cf. *Lk* 2:19, 51), and Mary of Bethany, who sat at the Lord's feet and listened attentively to his words (cf. *Lk* 10:38). I think in particular of monks and cloistered nuns, who by virtue of their separation from the world are all the more closely united to Christ, the heart of the world. More than ever, the Church needs the witness of men and women resolved to "put nothing before the love of Christ".[279] The world today is often excessively caught up in outward activities and risks losing its bearings. Contemplative men and women, by their lives of prayer, attentive hearing and

---

[278] Cf. *Propositio* 24.
[279] SAINT BENEDICT, *Rule*, IV, 21: SC 181, 456-458.

meditation on God's Word, remind us that man does not live by bread alone but by every word that comes from the mouth of God (cf. *Mt* 4:4). All the faithful, then, should be clearly conscious that this form of life "shows today's world what is most important, indeed, the one thing necessary: there is an ultimate reason which makes life worth living, and that is God and his inscrutable love".[280]

d) *The word of God and the lay faithful*

84.   The Synod frequently spoke of the laity and thanked them for their generous activity in spreading the Gospel in the various settings of daily life, at work and in the schools, in the family and in education.[281] This responsibility, rooted in Baptism, needs to develop through an ever more conscious Christian way of life capable of "accounting for the hope" within us (cf. *1 Pet* 3:15). In the *Gospel of Matthew*, Jesus points out that "the field is the world, and the good seed are the children of the Kingdom" (13:38). These words apply especially to the Christian laity, who live out their specific vocation to holiness by a life in the Spirit expressed "in a particular way by their *engagement in temporal matters* and by their *participation in earthly activities*".[282] The laity need to be trained

---

[280] BENEDICT XVI, *Address at Heiligenkreuz Abbey* (9 September 2007): AAS 99 (2007), 856.

[281] Cf. *Propositio* 30.

[282] JOHN PAUL II, Post-Synodal Apostolic Exhortation

to discern God's will through a familiarity with his word, read and studied in the Church under the guidance of her legitimate pastors. They can receive this training at the school of the great ecclesial spiritualities, all of which are grounded in sacred Scripture. Wherever possible, dioceses themselves should provide an opportunity for continuing formation to lay persons charged with particular ecclesial responsibilities.[283]

e) *The word of God, marriage and the family*

85.   The Synod also felt the need to stress the relationship between the word of God, marriage and the Christian family. Indeed, "with the proclamation of the word of God, the Church reveals to Christian families their true identity, what it is and what it must be in accordance with the Lord's plan".[284] Consequently, it must never be forgotten that *the word of God is at the very origin of marriage* (cf. *Gen* 2:24) and that Jesus himself made marriage one of the institutions of his Kingdom (cf. *Mt* 19:4-8), elevating to the dignity of a sacrament what was inscribed in human nature from the beginning. "In the celebration of the sacrament, a man and a woman speak a prophetic word of reciprocal self-giving, that of being 'one flesh', a

Christifideles Laici (30 December 1988), 17: AAS 81 (1989), 418.
    [283] Cf. *Propositio* 33.
    [284] JOHN PAUL II, Post-Synodal Apostolic Exhortation *Familiaris Consortio* (22 November 1981), 49: AAS 74 (1982), 140-141.

sign of the mystery of the union of Christ with the Church (cf. *Eph* 5:31-32)".[285] Fidelity to God's word leads us to point out that nowadays this institution is in many ways under attack from the current mentality. In the face of widespread confusion in the sphere of affectivity, and the rise of ways of thinking which trivialize the human body and sexual differentiation, the word of God reaffirms the original goodness of the human being, created as man and woman and called to a love which is faithful, reciprocal and fruitful.

The great mystery of marriage is the source of the essential *responsibility of parents towards their children*. Part of authentic parenthood is to pass on and bear witness to the meaning of life in Christ: through their fidelity and the unity of family life, spouses are the first to proclaim God's word to their children. The ecclesial community must support and assist them in fostering family prayer, attentive hearing of the word of God, and knowledge of the Bible. To this end the Synod urged that *every household have its Bible*, to be kept in a worthy place and used for reading and prayer. Whatever help is needed in this regard can be provided by priests, deacons and a well-prepared laity. The Synod also recommended the formation of small communities of families, where common prayer and meditation on passages of Scripture can be cultivated.[286] Spouses should also remem-

[285] *Propositio* 20.
[286] Cf. *Propositio* 21.

ber that "the Word of God is a precious support amid the difficulties which arise in marriage and in family life".[287]

Here I would like to highlight the recommendations of the Synod concerning the *role of women in relation to the word of God*. Today, more than in the past, the "feminine genius",[288] to use the words of John Paul II, has contributed greatly to the understanding of Scripture and to the whole life of the Church, and this is now also the case with biblical studies. The Synod paid special attention to the indispensable role played by women in the family, education, catechesis and the communication of values. "They have an ability to lead people to hear God's word, to enjoy a personal relationship with God, and to show the meaning of forgiveness and of evangelical sharing".[289] They are likewise messengers of love, models of mercy and peacemakers; they communicate warmth and humanity in a world which all too often judges people according to the ruthless criteria of exploitation and profit.

The prayerful reading of sacred Scripture and "lectio divina"

86. The Synod frequently insisted on the need for a prayerful approach to the sacred text as a

---

[287] *Propositio* 20.
[288] Cf. Apostolic Letter *Mulieris Dignitatem* (15 August 1988), 31: AAS 80 (1988), 1727-1729.
[289] *Propositio* 17.

fundamental element in the spiritual life of every believer, in the various ministries and states in life, with particular reference to *lectio divina*.[290] The word of God is at the basis of all authentic Christian spirituality. The Synod Fathers thus took up the words of the Dogmatic Constitution *Dei Verbum*: "Let the faithful go gladly to the sacred text itself, whether in the sacred liturgy, which is full of the divine words, or in devout reading, or in such suitable exercises and various other helps which, with the approval and guidance of the pastors of the Church, are happily spreading everywhere in our day. Let them remember, however, that prayer should accompany the reading of sacred Scripture".[291] The Council thus sought to reappropriate the great patristic tradition which had always recommended approaching the Scripture in dialogue with God. As Saint Augustine puts it: "Your prayer is the word you speak to God. When you read the Bible, God speaks to you; when you pray, you speak to God".[292] Origen, one of the great masters of this way of reading the Bible, maintains that understanding Scripture demands, even more than study, closeness to Christ and prayer. Origen was convinced, in fact, that the best way to know God is through love, and that there can be no authentic *scientia Christi* apart from growth in his love. In his

---

[290] *Propositiones* 9 and 22.

[291] No. 25.

[292] *Enarrationes in Psalmos*, 85, 7: PL 37, 1086.

Letter to Gregory, the great Alexandrian theologian gave this advice: "Devote yourself to the *lectio* of the divine Scriptures; apply yourself to this with perseverance. Do your reading with the intent of believing in and pleasing God. If during the *lectio* you encounter a closed door, knock and it will be opened to you by that guardian of whom Jesus said, 'The gatekeeper will open it for him'. By applying yourself in this way to *lectio divina*, search diligently and with unshakable trust in God for the meaning of the divine Scriptures, which is hidden in great fullness within. You ought not, however, to be satisfied merely with knocking and seeking: to understand the things of God, what is absolutely necessary is *oratio*. For this reason, the Saviour told us not only: 'Seek and you will find', and 'Knock and it shall be opened to you', but also added, 'Ask and you shall receive'".[293]

In this regard, however, one must *avoid the risk of an individualistic approach*, and remember that God's word is given to us precisely to build communion, to unite us in the Truth along our path to God. While it is a word addressed to each of us personally, it is also a word which builds community, which builds the Church. Consequently, *the sacred text must always be approached in the communion of the Church*. In effect, "a communal reading of Scripture is extremely important, because the living subject in the sacred Scriptures is the People of God, it is the Church… Scripture does not

---

[293] ORIGEN, *Epistola ad Gregorium*, 3: PG 11, 92.

belong to the past, because its subject, the People of God inspired by God himself, is always the same, and therefore the word is always alive in the living subject. As such, it is important to read and experience sacred Scripture in communion with the Church, that is, with all the great witnesses to this word, beginning with the earliest Fathers up to the saints of our own day, up to the present-day magisterium".[294]

For this reason, *the privileged place* for the prayerful reading of sacred Scripture *is the liturgy*, and particularly *the Eucharist*, in which, as we celebrate the Body and Blood of Christ in the sacrament, the word itself is present and at work in our midst. In some sense the prayerful reading of the Bible, personal and communal, must always be related to the Eucharistic celebration. Just as the adoration of the Eucharist prepares for, accompanies and follows the liturgy of the Eucharist,[295] so too prayerful reading, personal and communal, prepares for, accompanies and deepens what the Church celebrates when she proclaims the word in a liturgical setting. By so closely relating *lectio* and liturgy, we can better grasp the criteria which should guide this practice in the area of pastoral care and in the spiritual life of the People of God.

87.   The documents produced before and during the Synod mentioned a number of methods for a

---

[294]   BENEDICT XVI, *Address to the Students of the Roman Major Seminary* (19 February 2007): AAS 99 (2007), 253-254.
[295]   Cf. ID., Post-Synodal Apostolic Exhortation *Sacramentum Caritatis* (22 February 2007), 66; AAS 99 (2007), 155-156.

faith-filled and fruitful approach to sacred Scripture. Yet the greatest attention was paid to *lectio divina*, which is truly "capable of opening up to the faithful the treasures of God's word, but also of bringing about an encounter with Christ, the living word of God".[296] I would like here to review the basic steps of this procedure. It opens with the reading (*lectio*) of a text, which leads to a desire to understand its true content: w*hat does the biblical text say in itself?* Without this, there is always a risk that the text will become a pretext for never moving beyond our own ideas. Next comes meditation (*meditatio*), which asks: *what does the biblical text say to us?* Here, each person, individually but also as a member of the community, must let himself or herself be moved and challenged. Following this comes prayer (*oratio*), which asks the question: *what do we say to the Lord in response to his word?* Prayer, as petition, intercession, thanksgiving and praise, is the primary way by which the word transforms us. Finally, *lectio divina* concludes with contemplation (*contemplatio*), during which we take up, as a gift from God, his own way of seeing and judging reality, and ask ourselves *what conversion of mind, heart and life is the Lord asking of us?* In the *Letter to the Romans*, Saint Paul tells us: "Do not be conformed to this world, but be transformed by the renewal of your mind, that you may prove what is the will of God, what is good and acceptable and perfect" (12:2). Contemplation aims at creating

[296] *Final Message*, III, 9.

within us a truly wise and discerning vision of reality, as God sees it, and at forming within us "the mind of Christ" (1 *Cor* 2:16). The word of God appears here as a criterion for discernment: it is "living and active, sharper than any two-edged sword, piercing to the division of soul and spirit, of joints and marrow, and discerning the thoughts and intentions of the heart" (*Heb* 4:12). We do well also to remember that the process of *lectio divina* is not concluded until it arrives at action (*actio*), which moves the believer to make his or her life a gift for others in charity.

We find the supreme synthesis and fulfilment of this process in the Mother of God. For every member of the faithful Mary is the model of docile acceptance of God's word, for she "kept all these things, pondering them in her heart" (*Lk* 2:19; cf. 2:51); she discovered the profound bond which unites, in God's great plan, apparently disparate events, actions and things.[297]

I would also like to echo what the Synod proposed about the importance of the personal reading of Scripture, also as a practice allowing for the possibility, in accordance with the Church's usual conditions, of gaining an indulgence either for oneself or for the faithful departed.[298] The

---

[297]   *Ibid.*

[298]   "*Plenaria indulgentia* conceditur christifideli qui Sacram Scripturam, iuxta textum a competenti auctoritate adprobatum, cum veneratione divino eloquio debita et ad modum lectionis spiritalis, per dimidiam saltem horam legerit; si per minus tem-

practice of indulgences[299] implies the doctrine of the infinite merits of Christ – which the Church, as the minister of the redemption, dispenses and applies, but it also implies that of the communion of saints, and it teaches us that "to whatever degree we are united in Christ, we are united to one another, and the supernatural life of each one can be useful for the others".[300] From this standpoint, the reading of the word of God sustains us on our journey of penance and conversion, enables us to deepen our sense of belonging to the Church, and helps us to grow in familiarity with God. As Saint Ambrose puts it, "When we take up the sacred Scriptures in faith and read them with the Church, we walk once more with God in the Garden".[301]

The word of God and Marian prayer

88. Mindful of the inseparable bond between the word of God and Mary of Nazareth, along with the Synod Fathers I urge that Marian prayer be encouraged among the faithful, above all in life of families, since it is an aid to meditating on the holy mysteries found in the Scriptures. A most helpful aid, for example, is the individual or

pus id egerit *indulgentia* erit partialis": APOSTOLIC PENITENTIARY, *Enchiridion Indulgentiarum. Normae et Concessiones* (16 July 1999), 30, §1.

[299] Cf. *Catechism of the Catholic Church*, 1471-1479.

[300] PAUL VI, Apostolic Constitution *Indulgentiarum Doctrina* (1 January 1967): AAS 59 (1967), 18-19.

[301] Cf. *Epistula* 49, 3: PL 16, 1204A.

communal recitation of the Holy Rosary,[302] which ponders the mysteries of Christ's life in union with Mary,[303] and which Pope John Paul II wished to enrich with the mysteries of light.[304] It is fitting that the announcement of each mystery be accompanied by a brief biblical text pertinent to that mystery, so as to encourage the memorization of brief biblical passages relevant to the mysteries of Christ's life.

The Synod also recommended that the faithful be encouraged to pray the *Angelus*. This prayer, simple yet profound, allows us "to commemorate daily the mystery of the Incarnate Word".[305] It is only right that the People of God, families and communities of consecrated persons, be faithful to this Marian prayer traditionally recited at sunrise, midday and sunset. In the *Angelus* we ask God to grant that, through Mary's intercession, we may imitate her in doing his will and in welcoming his word into our lives. This practice can help us to grow in an authentic love for the mystery of the incarnation.

The ancient prayers of the Christian East which contemplate the entire history of salvation in the light of the *Theotokos*, the Mother of God,

---

[302] Cf. CONGREGATION FOR DIVINE WORSHIP AND THE DISCIPLINE OF THE SACRAMENTS, *Directory on Popular Piety and the Liturgy. Principles and Orientations* (17 December 2001), 197-202: *Enchiridion Vaticanum* 20, Nos. 2638-2643.

[303] Cf. *Propositio* 55.

[304] Cf. JOHN PAUL II, Apostolic Letter *Rosarium Virginis Mariae* (16 October 2002): AAS 95 (2003), 5-36.

[305] *Propositio* 55.

are likewise worthy of being known, appreciated and widely used. Here particular mention can be made of the *Akathist* and *Paraklesis* prayers. These hymns of praise, chanted in the form of a litany and steeped in the faith of the Church and in references to the Bible, help the faithful to meditate on the mysteries of Christ in union with Mary. In particular, the venerable *Akathist* hymn to the Mother of God – so-called because it is sung while standing – represents one of the highest expressions of the Marian piety of the Byzantine tradition.[306] Praying with these words opens wide the heart and disposes it to the peace that is from above, from God, to that peace which is Christ himself, born of Mary for our salvation.

The word of God and the Holy Land

89.   As we call to mind the Word of God who became flesh in the womb of Mary of Nazareth, our heart now turns to the land where the mystery of our salvation was accomplished, and from which the word of God spread to the ends of the earth. By the power of the Holy Spirit, the Word became flesh in a specific time and place, in a strip of land on the edges of the Roman Empire. The more we appreciate the universality and the uniqueness of Christ's person, the more we look with gratitude to that land where Jesus was

---

[306] Cf. CONGREGATION FOR DIVINE WORSHIP AND THE DISCIPLINE OF THE SACRAMENTS, *Directory on Popular Piety and the Liturgy. Principles and Orientations* (17 December 2001), 207: *Enchiridion Vaticanum* 20, Nos. 2656-2657.

born, where he lived and where he gave his life for us. The stones on which our Redeemer walked are still charged with his memory and continue to "cry out" the Good News. For this reason, the Synod Fathers recalled the felicitous phrase which speaks of the Holy Land as "the Fifth Gospel".[307] How important it is that in those places there be Christian communities, notwithstanding any number of hardships! The Synod of Bishops expressed profound closeness to all those Christians who dwell in the land of Jesus and bear witness to their faith in the Risen One. Christians there are called to serve not only as "a beacon of faith for the universal Church, but also as a leaven of harmony, wisdom, and equilibrium in the life of a society which traditionally has been, and continues to be, pluralistic, multi-ethnic and multireligious".[308]

The Holy Land today remains a goal of pilgrimage for the Christian people, a place of prayer and penance, as was testified to in antiquity by authors like Saint Jerome.[309] The more we turn our eyes and our hearts to the earthly Jerusalem, the more will our yearning be kindled for the heavenly Jerusalem, the true goal of every pilgrimage, along with our eager desire that the name of Jesus, the one name which brings salvation, may be acknowledged by all (cf. *Acts* 4:12).

[307] Cf. *Propositio* 51.

[308] BENEDICT XVI, *Homily at Mass in the Valley of Josaphat, Jerusalem* (12 May 2009): AAS 101 (2009), 473.

[309] Cf. *Epistola* 108, 14: CSEL 55, pp. 324-325.

PART THREE

VERBUM MUNDO

"No one has ever seen God. It is God the only Son,
who is close to the Father's heart,
who has made him known"
(Jn 1:18)

The Church's Mission: to Proclaim the Word of God to the World

The Word from the Father and to the Father

90.   Saint John powerfully expresses the fundamental paradox of the Christian faith. On the one hand, he says that "no one has ever seen God" (*Jn* 1:18; cf. 1 *Jn* 4:12). In no way can our imaginations, our concepts or our words ever define or embrace the infinite reality of the Most High. He remains *Deus semper maior*. Yet Saint John also tells us that the Word truly "became flesh" (*Jn* 1:14). The only-begotten Son, who is ever with the Father, has made known the God whom "no one has ever seen" (*Jn* 1:18). Jesus Christ comes to us, "full of grace and truth" (*Jn* 1:14), to give us these gifts (cf. *Jn* 1:17); and "from his fullness we have all received, grace upon grace" (*Jn* 1:16). In the Prologue of his Gospel, John thus contemplates the Word from his being with God to his becoming flesh and his return to the Father with our humanity, which he has assumed for ever. In this coming forth from God and returning to him (cf. *Jn* 13:3; 16:28; 17:8,10), Christ is presented as the one who "tells us" about God (cf. *Jn* 1:18). Indeed, as Saint Irenaeus of Lyons says, the Son "is

the revealer of the Father".[310] Jesus of Nazareth is, so to speak, the "exegete" of the God whom "no one has ever seen". "He is the image of the invisible God" (*Col* 1:15). Here we see fulfilled the prophecy of Isaiah about the effectiveness of the Lord's word: as the rain and snow come down from heaven to water and to make the earth fruitful, so too the word of God "shall not return to me empty, but it shall accomplish that which I purpose, and prosper in the thing for which I sent it" (cf. *Is* 55:10f.). Jesus Christ is this definitive and effective word which came forth from the Father and returned to him, perfectly accomplishing his will in the world.

Proclaiming to the world the "Logos" of hope

91.   The word of God has bestowed upon us the divine life which transfigures the face of the earth, making all things new (cf. *Rev* 21:5). His word engages us not only as *hearers* of divine revelation, but also as its *heralds*. The one whom the Father has sent to do his will (cf. *Jn* 5:36-38; 6:38-40; 7:16-18) draws us to himself and makes us part of his life and mission. The Spirit of the Risen Lord empowers us to proclaim the word everywhere by the witness of our lives. This was experienced by the first Christian community, which saw the word spread through preaching and witness (cf. *Acts* 6:7). Here we can think in particular of the life of the Apostle Paul, a man

---

[310] *Adversus Haereses*, IV, 20, 7: PG 7, 1037.

completely caught up by the Lord (cf. *Phil* 3:12) – "it is no longer I who live, but Christ who lives in me" (*Gal* 2:20) – and by his mission: "woe to me if I do not proclaim the Gospel!" (*1 Cor* 9:16). Paul knew well that what was revealed in Christ is really salvation for all peoples, liberation from the slavery of sin in order to enjoy the freedom of the children of God.

What the Church proclaims to the world is the *Logos of Hope* (cf. *1 Pet* 3:15); in order to be able to live fully each moment, men and women need "the great hope" which is "the God who possesses a human face and who 'has loved us to the end' (*Jn* 13:1)".[311] This is why the Church is missionary by her very nature. We cannot keep to ourselves the words of eternal life given to us in our encounter with Jesus Christ: they are meant for everyone, for every man and woman. Everyone today, whether he or she knows it or not, needs this message. May the Lord himself, as in the time of the prophet Amos, raise up in our midst a new hunger and thirst for the word of God (cf. *Am* 8:11). It is our responsibility to pass on what, by God's grace, we ourselves have received.

The word of God is the source of the Church's mission

92.   The Synod of Bishops forcefully reaffirmed the need within the Church for a revival of the

---

[311] BENEDICT XVI, Encyclical Letter *Spe Salvi* (30 November 2007), 31: AAS 99 (2007), 1010.

missionary consciousness present in the People of God from the beginning. The first Christians saw their missionary preaching as a necessity rooted in the very nature of faith: the God in whom they believed was the God of all, the one true God who revealed himself in Israel's history and ultimately in his Son, who thus provided the response which, in their inmost being, all men and women awaited. The first Christian communities felt that their faith was not part of a particular cultural tradition, differing from one people to another, but belonged instead to the realm of truth, which concerns everyone equally.

Once more it is Saint Paul who, by his life, illustrates the meaning of the Christian mission and its fundamental universality. We can think here of the episode related in the *Acts of the Apostles* about the Athenian Areopagus (cf. 17:16-34). The Apostle of the Nations enters into dialogue with people of various cultures precisely because he is conscious that the mystery of God, Known yet Unknown, which every man and woman perceives, however confusedly, has really been revealed in history: "What therefore you worship as unknown, this I proclaim to you" (*Acts* 17:23). In fact, the newness of Christian proclamation is that we can tell all peoples: "God has shown himself. In person. And now the way to him is open. The novelty of the Christian message does not consist in an idea but in a fact: God has revealed himself".[312]

[312] BENEDICT XVI, *Address to Representatives of the World of*

93.   Consequently, the Church's mission cannot be considered as an optional or supplementary element in her life. Rather it entails letting the Holy Spirit assimilate us to Christ himself, and thus to share in his own mission: "As the Father has sent me, so I send you" (*Jn* 20:21) to share the word with your entire life. It is the word itself which impels us towards our brothers and sisters: it is the word which illuminates, purifies, converts; we are only its servants.

We need, then, to discover ever anew the urgency and the beauty of the proclamation of the word for the coming of the Kingdom of God which Christ himself preached. Thus we grow in the realization, so clear to the Fathers of the Church, that the proclamation of the word has as its content the Kingdom of God (cf. *Mk* 1:14-15), which, in the memorable phrase of Origen,[313] *is the very person of Jesus (Autobasileia)*. The Lord offers salvation to men and women in every age. All of us recognize how much the light of Christ needs to illumine every area of human life: the family, schools, culture, work, leisure and the other aspects of social life.[314] It

Culture at the "Collège des Bernardins" in Paris (12 September 2008): AAS 100 (2008), 730.

[313] Cf. *In Evangelium secundum Matthaeum* 17:7: PG 13, 1197B; SAINT JEROME, *Translatio homiliarum Origenis in Lucam*, 36: PL 26, 324-325.

[314] Cf. BENEDICT XVI, *Homily for the Opening of the Twelfth Ordinary General Assembly of the Synod of Bishops* (5 October 2008): AAS 100 (2008), 757.

is not a matter of preaching a word of consolation, but rather a word which disrupts, which calls to conversion and which opens the way to an encounter with the one through whom a new humanity flowers.

All the baptized are responsible for this proclamation

94.   Since the entire People of God is a people which has been "sent", the Synod reaffirmed that "the mission of proclaiming the word of God is the task of all of the disciples of Jesus Christ based on their Baptism".[315] No believer in Christ can feel dispensed from this responsibility which comes from the fact of our sacramentally belonging to the Body of Christ. A consciousness of this must be revived in every family, parish, community, association and ecclesial movement. The Church, as a mystery of communion, is thus entirely missionary, and everyone, according to his or her proper state in life, is called to give an incisive contribution to the proclamation of Christ.

Bishops and *priests*, in accordance with their specific mission, are the first to be called to live a life completely at the service of the word, to proclaim the Gospel, to celebrate the sacraments and to form the faithful in the authentic knowledge of Scripture. *Deacons* too must feel themselves called to cooperate, in accordance with their specific mission, in this task of evangelization.

[315] *Propositio* 38.

Throughout the Church's history *the consecrated life* has been outstanding for explicitly taking up the task of proclaiming and preaching the word of God in the *missio ad gentes* and in the most difficult situations, for being ever ready to adapt to new situations and for setting out courageously and boldly along fresh paths in meeting new challenges for the effective proclamation of God's word.[316]

The *laity* are called to exercise their own prophetic role, which derives directly from their Baptism, and to bear witness to the Gospel in daily life, wherever they find themselves. In this regard the Synod Fathers expressed "the greatest esteem, gratitude and encouragement for the service to evangelization which so many of the lay faithful, and women in particular, provide with generosity and commitment in their communities throughout the world, following the example of Mary Magdalene, the first witness of the joy of Easter".[317] The Synod also recognized with gratitude that the ecclesial movements and the new communities are a great force for evangelization in our times and an incentive to the development of new ways of proclaiming the Gospel.[318]

[316] Cf. CONGREGATION FOR INSTITUTES OF CONSECRATED LIFE AND FOR SOCIETIES OF APOSTOLIC LIFE, Instruction *Starting Afresh from Christ: A Renewed Commitment to Consecrated Life in the Third Millennium* (19 May 2002), 36: *Enchiridion Vaticanum* 21, Nos. 488-491.

[317] *Propositio* 30.

[318] Cf. *Propositio* 38.

The necessity of the "missio ad gentes"

95.   In calling upon all the faithful to proclaim God's word, the Synod Fathers restated the need in our day too for a decisive commitment to the *missio ad gentes*. In no way can the Church restrict her pastoral work to the "ordinary maintenance" of those who already know the Gospel of Christ. Missionary outreach is a clear sign of the maturity of an ecclesial community. The Fathers also insisted that the word of God is the saving truth which men and women in every age need to hear. For this reason, it must be explicitly proclaimed. The Church must go out to meet each person in the strength of the Spirit (cf. *1 Cor* 2:5) and continue her prophetic defence of people's right and freedom to hear the word of God, while constantly seeking out the most effective ways of proclaiming that word, even at the risk of persecution.[319] The Church feels duty-bound to proclaim to every man and woman the word that saves (cf. *Rom* 1:14).

Proclamation and the new evangelization

96.   Pope John Paul II, taking up the prophetic words of Pope Paul VI in the Apostolic Exhortation *Evangelii Nuntiandi*, had in a variety of ways reminded the faithful of the need for a new missionary season for the entire people of God.[320]

[319] Cf. *Propositio* 49.
[320] Cf. JOHN PAUL II, Encyclical Letter *Redemptoris Missio*

158

At the dawn of the third millennium not only are there still many peoples who have not come to know the Good News, but also a great many Christians who need to have the word of God once more persuasively proclaimed to them, so that they can concretely experience the power of the Gospel. Many of our brothers and sisters are "baptized, but insufficiently evangelized".[321] In a number of cases, nations once rich in faith and in vocations are losing their identity under the influence of a secularized culture.[322] The need for a new evangelization, so deeply felt by my venerable Predecessor, must be valiantly reaffirmed, in the certainty that God's word is effective. The Church, sure of her Lord's fidelity, never tires of proclaiming the good news of the Gospel and invites all Christians to discover anew the attraction of following Christ.

The word of God and Christian witness

97.   The immense horizons of the Church's mission and the complexity of today's situation call for new ways of effectively communicating the word of God. The Holy Spirit, the protagonist of all evangelization, will never fail to guide Christ's

(7 December 1990): AAS 83 (1991), 294-340; Apostolic Letter *Novo Millennio Ineunte* (6 January 2001), 40: AAS 93 (2001), 294-295.

    [321] *Propositio* 38.

    [322] Cf. BENEDICT XVI, *Homily for the Opening of the Twelfth Ordinary General Assembly of the Synod of Bishops* (5 October 2008): AAS 100 (2008), 753-757.

Church in this activity. Yet it is important that every form of proclamation keep in mind, first of all, the intrinsic relationship between *the communication of God's word* and *Christian witness*. The very credibility of our proclamation depends on this. On the one hand, the word must communicate everything that the Lord himself has told us. On the other hand, it is indispensable, through witness, to make this word credible, lest it appear merely as a beautiful philosophy or utopia, rather than a reality that can be lived and itself give life. This reciprocity between word and witness reflects the way in which God himself communicated through the incarnation of his Word. The word of God reaches men and women "through an encounter with witnesses who make it present and alive".[323] In a particular way, young people need to be introduced to the word of God "through encounter and authentic witness by adults, through the positive influence of friends and the great company of the ecclesial community".[324]

There is a close relationship between the testimony of Scripture, as the self-attestation of God's word, and the witness given by the lives of believers. One implies and leads to the other. Christian witness communicates the word attested in the Scriptures. For their part, the Scriptures explain the witness which Christians are called to give by their lives. Those who encounter cred-

[323] *Propositio* 38.
[324] *Final Message*, IV, 12.

ible witnesses of the Gospel thus come to realize how effective God's word can be in those who receive it.

98.   In this interplay between witness and word we can understand what Pope Paul VI stated in the Apostolic Exhortation *Evangelii Nuntiandi*. Our responsibility is not limited to suggesting shared values to the world; rather, we need to arrive at an explicit proclamation of the word of God. Only in this way will we be faithful to Christ's mandate: "The Good News proclaimed by the witness of life sooner or later has to be proclaimed by the word of life. There is no true evangelization unless the name, the teaching, the life, the promises, the Kingdom and the mystery of Jesus of Nazareth, the Son of God, are proclaimed".[325]

The fact that the proclamation of the word of God calls for the testimony of one's life is a datum clearly present in the Christian consciousness from the beginning. Christ himself is the faithful and true witness (cf. *Acts* 1:5; 3:14), it is he who testifies to the Truth (cf. *Jn* 18:37). Here I would like to echo the countless testimonials which we had the grace of hearing during the synodal assembly. We were profoundly moved to hear the stories of those who lived their faith and bore outstanding witness to the Gospel even under regimes hostile to Christianity or in situations of persecution.

[325] PAUL VI, Apostolic Exhortation *Evangelii Nuntiandi* (8 December 1975), 22: AAS 68 (1976), 20.

None of this should cause us fear. Jesus himself said to his disciples: "A servant is not greater than his master. If they persecuted me, they will persecute you" (*Jn* 15:20). For this reason I would like, with the whole Church, to lift up to God a hymn of praise for the witness of our many faithful brothers and sisters who, even in our day, have given their lives to communicate the truth of God's love revealed to us in the crucified and risen Christ. I also express the whole Church's gratitude for those Christians who have not yielded in the face of obstacles and even persecutions for the sake of the Gospel. We likewise embrace with deep fraternal affection the faithful of all those Christian communities, particularly in Asia and in Africa, who presently risk their life or social segregation because of their faith. Here we encounter the true spirit of the Gospel, which proclaims blessed those who are persecuted on account of the Lord Jesus (cf. *Mt* 5:11). In so doing, we once more call upon the governments of nations to guarantee everyone freedom of conscience and religion, as well as the ability to express their faith publicly.[326]

THE WORD OF GOD
AND COMMITMENT IN THE WORLD

Serving Jesus in "the least of his brethren" (Mt 25:40)

99.   The word of God sheds light on human existence and stirs our conscience to take a deeper

---

[326] Cf. SECOND VATICAN ECUMENICAL COUNCIL, Declaration on Religious Freedom *Dignitatis Humanae*, 2 and 7.

look at our lives, inasmuch as all human history stands under God's judgment: "When the Son of Man comes in his glory, and all the angels with him, then he will sit on his glorious throne. Before him will be gathered all the nations" (*Mt* 25:31-32). Nowadays we tend to halt in a superficial way before the importance of the passing moment, as if it had nothing to do with the future. The Gospel, on the other hand, reminds us that every moment of our life is important and must be lived intensely, in the knowledge that everyone will have to give an account of his or her life. In the twenty-fifth chapter of the *Gospel of Matthew*, the Son of Man considers whatever we do or do not do to "the least of his brethren" (cf. 25:40, 45) as done or not done to himself: "I was hungry and you gave me food, I was thirsty and you gave me drink, I was a stranger and you welcomed me, I was naked and you clothed me, I was sick and you visited me, I was in prison and you came to me" (25:35-36). The word of God itself emphasizes the need for our engagement in the world and our responsibility before Christ, the Lord of history. As we proclaim the Gospel, let us encourage one another to do good and to commit ourselves to justice, reconciliation and peace.

The word of God and commitment to justice in society

100.   God's word inspires men and women to build relationships based on rectitude and justice, and testifies to the great value in God's eyes of

every effort to create a more just and more liveable world.[327] The word of God itself unambiguously denounces injustices and promotes solidarity and equality.[328] In the light of the Lord's words, let us discern the "signs of the times" present in history, and not flee from a commitment to those who suffer and the victims of forms of selfishness. The Synod recalled that a commitment to justice and to changing our world is an essential element of evangelization. In the words of Pope Paul VI, we must "reach and as it were overturn with the force of the Gospel the standards of judgement, the interests, the thought-patterns, the sources of inspiration and life-styles of humanity that are in contrast with the word of God and with his plan for salvation".[329]

For this reason, the Synod Fathers wished to say a special word to all those who take part in political and social life. Evangelization and the spread of God's word ought to inspire their activity in the world, as they work for the true common good in respecting and promoting the dignity of every person. Certainly it is not the direct task of the Church to create a more just society, although she does have the right and duty to intervene on ethical and moral issues related to the good of individuals and peoples. It is primarily the task of the lay faithful, formed in the school of the Gos-

[327] Cf. *Propositio* 39.

[328] Cf. BENEDICT XVI, *Message for the 2009 World Day of Peace* (8 December 2008): *Insegnamenti* IV, 2 (2008), 792-802.

[329] Apostolic Exhortation *Evangelii Nuntiandi* (8 December 1975), 19: AAS 68 (1976), 18.

pel, to be directly involved in political and social activity. For this reason, the Synod recommends that they receive a suitable formation in the principles of the Church's social teaching.[330]

101.   I would like also to call the attention of everyone to the importance of defending and promoting the *human rights of every person*, based on the natural law written on the human heart, which, as such, are "universal, inviolable and inalienable".[331] The Church expresses the hope that by the recognition of these rights human dignity will be more effectively acknowledged and universally promoted,[332] inasmuch as it is a distinctive mark imprinted by the Creator on his creatures, taken up and redeemed by Jesus Christ through his incarnation, death and resurrection. The spread of the word of God cannot fail to strengthen the recognition of, and respect for, the human rights of every person.[333]

The proclamation of God's word, reconciliation and peace between peoples

102.   Among the many areas where commitment is needed, the Synod earnestly called for

---

[330] Cf. *Propositio* 39.

[331] JOHN XXIII, Encyclical Letter *Pacem in Terris* (11 April 1963), 1: AAS 55 (1963), 259.

[332] JOHN PAUL II, Encyclical letter *Centesimus Annus* (1 May 1991), 47: AAS 83 (1991), 851-852; *Address to the General Assembly of the United Nations* (2 October 1979), 13: AAS 71 (1979), 1152-1153.

[333] Cf. *Compendium of the Social Doctrine of the Church*, 152-159.

the promotion of reconciliation and peace. In the present context it is more necessary than ever to rediscover the word of God as a source of reconciliation and peace, since in that word God is reconciling to himself all things (cf. *2 Cor* 5:18-20; *Eph* 1:10): Christ "is our peace" (*Eph* 2:14), the one who breaks down the walls of division. A number of interventions at the Synod documented the grave and violent conflicts and tensions present on our planet. At times these hostilities seem to take on the appearance of interreligious conflict. Here I wish to affirm once more that religion can never justify intolerance or war. We cannot kill in God's name![334] Each religion must encourage the right use of reason and promote ethical values that consolidate civil coexistence.

In fidelity to the work of reconciliation accomplished by God in Jesus Christ crucified and risen, Catholics and men and women of goodwill must commit themselves to being an example of reconciliation for the building of a just and peaceful society.[335] We should never forget that "where human words become powerless because the tragic clash of violence and arms prevails, the prophetic power of God's word does not waver, reminding us that peace is possible and that we ourselves must be instruments of reconciliation and peace".[336]

---

[334] Cf. BENEDICT XVI, *Message for the 2007 World Day of Peace* (8 December 2006), 10: *Insegnamenti* II, 2 (2006), 780.

[335] Cf. *Propositio* 8.

[336] BENEDICT XVI, *Homily* (25 January 2009): *Insegnamenti* V, 1 (2009), 141.

103.   Commitment to justice, reconciliation and peace finds its ultimate foundation and fulfilment in the love revealed to us in Christ. By listening to the testimonies offered during the Synod, we saw more clearly the bond between a love-filled hearing of God's word and selfless service of our brothers and sisters; all believers should see the need to "translate the word that we have heard into gestures of love, because this is the only way to make the Gospel proclamation credible, despite the human weakness that marks individuals".[337] Jesus passed through this world doing good (cf. *Acts* 10:38). Listening with docility to the word of God in the Church awakens "charity and justice towards all, especially towards the poor".[338] We should never forget that "love – *caritas* – will always prove necessary, even in the most just society ... whoever wants to eliminate love is preparing to eliminate man as such".[339] I therefore encourage the faithful to meditate often on the Apostle Paul's hymn to charity and to draw inspiration from it: "Love is patient and kind; love is not jealous or boastful; it is not arrogant or rude. Love does not insist on its own way; it is not irritable or resentful; it does not rejoice at wrong

---

[337] ID., *Homily at the Conclusion of the Twelfth Ordinary General Assembly of the Synod of Bishops* (26 October 2008): AAS 100 (2008), 779.

[338] *Propositio* 11.

[339] BENEDICT XVI, Encyclical letter *Deus Caritas Est* (25 December 2005), 28: AAS 98 (2006), 240.

but delights in the truth. Love bears all things, believes all things, hopes all things, endures all things. Love never ends" (*1 Cor* 13:4-8).

Love of neighbour, rooted in the love of God, ought to see us constantly committed as individuals and as an ecclesial community, both local and universal. As Saint Augustine says: "It is essential to realize that love is the fullness of the Law, as it is of all the divine Scriptures … Whoever claims to have understood the Scriptures, or any part of them, without striving as a result to grow in this twofold love of God and neighbour, makes it clear that he has not yet understood them".[340]

The proclamation of the word of God and young people

104.   The Synod paid particular attention to the proclamation of God's word to the younger generation. Young people are already active members of the Church and they represent its future. Often we encounter in them a spontaneous openness to hearing the word of God and a *sincere desire to know Jesus*. Youth is a time when genuine and irrepressible *questions* arise about the meaning of life and the direction our own lives should take. Only God can give the true answer to these questions. Concern for young people calls for courage and clarity in the message we proclaim; we need to help young people to gain confidence and fa-

[340] *De Doctrina Christiana*, I, 35, 39 – 36, 40: PL 34, 34.

miliarity with sacred Scripture so it can become a compass pointing out the path to follow.[341] Young people need witnesses and teachers who can walk with them, teaching them to love the Gospel and to share it, especially with their peers, and thus to become authentic and credible messengers.[342]

God's word needs to be presented in a way that brings out its implications for each person's vocation and assists young people in choosing the direction they will give to their lives, including that of total consecration to God.[343] Authentic vocations to the consecrated life and to the priesthood find fertile ground in a faith-filled contact with the word of God. I repeat once again the appeal I made at the beginning of my pontificate to open wide the doors to Christ: "If we let Christ into our lives, we lose nothing, nothing, absolutely nothing of what makes life free, beautiful and great. No! Only in this friendship are the doors of life opened wide. Only in this friendship is the great potential of human existence truly revealed. … Dear young people: do not be afraid of Christ! He takes nothing away and he gives you everything. When we give ourselves to him, we receive a hundredfold in return. Yes, open, open wide the doors to Christ – and you will find true life".[344]

[341] Cf. BENEDICT XVI, *Message for the Twenty-first World Youth Day* (22 February 2006): AAS 98 (2006), 282-286.
[342] Cf. *Propositio* 34.
[343] Cf. *ibid.*
[344] *Homily* (24 April 2005): AAS 97 (2005), 712.

105.   The word of God makes us attentive to history and to emerging realities. In considering the Church's mission of evangelization, the Synod thus decided to address as well the complex phenomenon of movements of migration, which in recent years have taken on unprecedented proportions. This issue is fraught with extremely delicate questions about the *security* of nations and the *welcome* to be given to those seeking refuge or improved conditions of living, health and work. Large numbers of people who know nothing of Christ, or who have an inadequate understanding of him, are settling in countries of Christian tradition. At the same time, persons from nations deeply marked by Christian faith are emigrating to countries where Christ needs to be proclaimed and a new evangelization is demanded. These situations offer new possibilities for the spread of God's word. In this regard the Synod Fathers stated that migrants are entitled to hear the *kerygma*, which is to be proposed, not imposed. If they are Christians, they require forms of pastoral care which can enable them to grow in the faith and to become in turn messengers of the Gospel. Taking into account the complexity of the phenomenon, a mobilization of all dioceses involved is essential, so that movements of migration will also be seen as an opportunity to discover new forms of presence and proclamation. It is also necessary that they ensure, to the extent possible, that

these our brothers and sisters receive adequate welcome and attention, so that, touched by the Good News, they will be able to be heralds of God's word and witnesses to the Risen Jesus, the hope of the world.[345]

The proclamation of the word of God and the suffering

106.   During the work of the Synod, the Fathers also considered the need to proclaim God's word to all those who are suffering, whether physically, psychologically or spiritually. It is in times of pain that *the ultimate questions about the meaning of one's life* make themselves acutely felt. If human words seem to fall silent before the mystery of evil and suffering, and if our society appears to value life only when it corresponds to certain standards of efficiency and well-being, the word of God makes us see that even these moments are mysteriously "embraced" by God's love. Faith born of an encounter with God's word helps us to realize that *human life deserves to be lived fully, even when weakened by illness and pain*. God created us for happiness and for life, whereas sickness and death came into the world as a result of sin (cf. *Wis* 2:23-24). Yet the Father of life is mankind's physician *par excellence*, and he does not cease to bend lovingly over suffering humanity. We contemplate the culmination of God's closeness to our sufferings in Jesus himself, "the Word incarnate. He suffered and

---

[345] Cf. *Propositio* 38.

died for us. By his passion and death he took our weakness upon himself and totally transformed it".[346]

Jesus' closeness to those who suffer is constant: it is prolonged in time thanks to the working of the Holy Spirit in the mission of the Church, in the word and in the sacraments, in men and women of good will, and in charitable initiatives undertaken with fraternal love by communities, thus making known God's true face and his love. The Synod thanked God for the luminous witness, often hidden, of all the many Christians – priests, religious and lay faithful – who have lent and continue to lend their hands, eyes and hearts to Christ, the true physician of body and soul. It exhorts all to continue to care for the infirm and to bring them the life-giving presence of the Lord Jesus in the word and in the Eucharist. Those who suffer should be helped to read the Scriptures and to realize that their condition itself enables them to share in a special way in Christ's redemptive suffering for the salvation of the world (cf. *2 Cor* 4:8-11,14).[347]

The proclamation of the word of God and the poor

107.   Sacred Scripture manifests God's special love for the poor and the needy (cf. *Mt* 25:31-46). The Synod Fathers frequently spoke of the

---

[346] BENEDICT XVI, *Homily for the Seventeenth World Day of the Sick* (11 February 2009): *Insegnamenti* V, 1 (2009), 232.
[347] Cf. *Propositio* 35.

importance of enabling these, our brothers and sisters, to hear the Gospel message and to experience the closeness of their pastors and communities. Indeed, "the poor are the first ones entitled to hear the proclamation of the Gospel; they need not only bread, but also words of life".[348] The diaconia of charity, which must never be lacking in our churches, should always be bound to the proclamation of the word and the celebration of the sacred mysteries.[349] Yet we also need to recognize and appreciate the fact that the poor are themselves agents of evangelization. In the Bible, the true poor are those who entrust themselves totally to God; in the Gospel Jesus calls them *blessed*, "for theirs is the Kingdom of Heaven" (*Mt* 5:3; cf. *Lk* 6:20). The Lord exalts the simplicity of heart of those who find in God true riches, placing their hope in him, and not in the things of this world. The Church cannot let the poor down: "Pastors are called to listen to them, to learn from them, to guide them in their faith and to encourage them to take responsibility for lives".[350]

The Church also knows that poverty can exist as a *virtue*, to be cultivated and chosen freely, as so many saints have done. Poverty can likewise exist as *indigence*, often due to injustice or selfishness, marked by hunger and need, and as a source

---

[348] *Propositio* 11.

[349] Cf. BENEDICT XVI, Encyclical Letter *Deus Caritas Est* (25 December 2005), 25: AAS 98 (2006), 236-237.

[350] *Propositio* 11.

of conflict. In her proclamation of God's word, the Church knows that a "virtuous circle" must be promoted between the poverty which is *to be chosen* and the poverty which is *to be combated*; we need to rediscover "moderation and solidarity, these values of the Gospel that are also universal … This entails decisions marked by justice and moderation".[351]

The proclamation of the word of God and the protection of creation

108.   Engagement with the world, as demanded by God's word, makes us look with new eyes at the entire created cosmos, which contains traces of that Word through whom all things were made (cf. *Jn* 1:2). As men and women who believe in and proclaim the Gospel, we have a responsibility towards creation. Revelation makes known God's plan for the cosmos, yet it also leads us to denounce that mistaken attitude which refuses to view all created realities as a reflection of their Creator, but instead as mere raw material, to be exploited without scruple. Man thus lacks that essential humility which would enable him to see creation as a gift from God, to be received and used in accordance with his plan. Instead, the arrogance of human beings who live "as if God did not exist" leads them to exploit and disfigure

[351] BENEDICT XVI, *Homily* (1 January 2009): *Insegnamenti* V, 1 (2009), 236-237.

nature, failing to see it as the handiwork of the creative word. In this theological context, I would like to echo the statements of the Synod Fathers who reminded us that "accepting the word of God, attested to by Scripture and by the Church's living Tradition, gives rise to a new way of seeing things, promotes an authentic ecology which has its deepest roots in the obedience of faith … [and] develops a renewed theological sensitivity to the goodness of all things, which are created in Christ".[352] We need to be re-educated in wonder and in the ability to recognize the beauty made manifest in created realities.[353]

THE WORD OF GOD AND CULTURE

The value of culture for the life of humanity

109.   Saint John's proclamation that the Word became flesh reveals the inseparable bond between *God's word* and the *human words* by which he communicates with us. In this context the Synod Fathers considered the relationship between the word of God and culture. God does not reveal himself in the abstract, but by using languages, imagery and expressions that are bound to different cultures. This relationship has proved fruitful, as the history of the Church abundantly testifies.

[352] *Propositio* 54.
[353] Cf. BENEDICT XVI, Post-Synodal Apostolic Exhortation *Sacramentum Caritatis* (22 February 2007), 92: AAS 99 (2007), 176-177.

Today it is entering a new phase due to the spread of the Gospel and its taking root within different cultures, as well as more recent developments in the culture of the West. It calls in the first place for a recognition of the importance of culture as such for the life of every man and woman. The phenomenon of culture is, in its various aspects, an essential datum of human experience. "Man lives always according to a culture which is properly his, and which in turn creates among persons a bond which is properly theirs, one which determines the inter-human and social character of human existence".[354]

Down the centuries the word of God has inspired different cultures, giving rise to fundamental moral values, outstanding expressions of art and exemplary life-styles.[355] Hence, in looking to a renewed encounter between the Bible and culture, I wish to reassure all those who are part of the world of culture that they have nothing to fear from openness to God's word, which never destroys true culture, but rather is a constant stimulus to seek ever more appropriate, meaningful and humane forms of expression. Every authentic culture, if it is truly to be at the service of humanity, has to be open to transcendence and, in the end, to God.

[354] JOHN PAUL II, *Address to UNESCO* (2 June 1980), 6: AAS 72 (1980), 738.
[355] Cf. *Propositio* 41.

110.   The Synod Fathers greatly stressed the importance of promoting a suitable knowledge of the Bible among those engaged in the area of culture, also in secularized contexts and among non-believers.[356] Sacred Scripture contains anthropological and philosophical values that have had a positive influence on humanity as a whole.[357] A sense of the Bible as a great code for cultures needs to be fully recovered.

Knowledge of the Bible in schools and universities

111.   One particular setting for an encounter between the word of God and culture is that of schools and universities. Pastors should be especially attentive to this milieu, promoting a deeper knowledge of the Bible and a grasp of its fruitful cultural implications also for the present day. Study centres supported by Catholic groups offer a distinct contribution to the promotion of culture and education – and this ought to be recognized. Nor must *religious education* be neglected, and religion teachers should be given careful training. Religious education is often the sole opportunity available for students to encounter the message of faith. In the teaching of religion, emphasis should be laid on knowledge of sacred

[356] Cf. *ibid.*
[357] JOHN PAUL II, Encyclical Letter *Fides et Ratio* (14 September 1998), 80: AAS 91 (1999), 67-68.

Scripture, as a means of overcoming prejudices old and new, and enabling its truth to be better known.[358]

Sacred Scripture in the variety of artistic expressions

112.   The relationship between the word of God and culture has found expression in many areas, especially in *the arts*. For this reason the great tradition of East and West has always esteemed works of art inspired by sacred Scripture, as for example the figurative arts and architecture, literature and music. I think too of the ancient language expressed by *icons*, which from the Eastern tradition is gradually spreading throughout the world. With the Synod Fathers, the whole Church expresses her appreciation, esteem and admiration of those artists "enamoured of beauty" who have drawn inspiration from the sacred texts. They have contributed to the decoration of our churches, to the celebration of our faith, to the enrichment of our liturgy and many of them have helped to make somehow perceptible, in time and space, realities that are unseen and eternal.[359] I encourage the competent offices and groups to promote in the Church a solid formation of artists with regard to sacred Scripture in the light of the Church's living Tradition and her magisterium.

[358] Cf. *Lineamenta* 23.
[359] Cf. *Propositio* 40.

113.   Linked to the relationship between the word of God and culture is the need for a careful and intelligent use of the communications media, both old and new. The Synod Fathers called for a proper knowledge of these media; they noted their rapid development and different levels of interaction, and asked for greater efforts to be made in gaining expertise in the various sectors involved, particularly in the *new media*, such as the *internet*. The Church already has a significant presence in the world of mass communications, and her magisterium has frequently intervened on the subject, beginning with the Second Vatican Council.[360] Discovering new methods of transmitting the Gospel message is part of the continuing evangelizing outreach of those who believe. Communications today take place through a worldwide network, and thus give new meaning to Christ's words: "What I tell you in the dark, utter in the light; and what you hear whispered, proclaim upon the housetops" (*Mt* 10:27). God's word should resound not only in the print media,

---

[360] Cf. SECOND VATICAN ECUMENICAL COUNCIL, Decree on the Instruments of Social Communication *Inter Mirifica*; PONTIFICAL COUNCIL FOR SOCIAL COMMUNICATIONS, Pastoral Instruction *Communio et Progressio* (23 May 1971): AAS 63 (1971), 596-656; JOHN PAUL II, Apostolic Letter *The Rapid Development* (24 January 2005): AAS 97 (2005) 265-274; PONTIFICAL COUNCIL FOR SOCIAL COMMUNICATIONS, Pastoral Instruction *Aetatis novae* (22 February 1992): AAS 84 (1992), 447-468; *The Church and Internet* (22 February 2002): *Enchiridion Vaticanum* 21, Nos. 66-95; *Ethics in Internet* (22 February 2002): *Enchiridion Vaticanum* 21, Nos. 96-127.

but in other forms of communication as well.[361] For this reason, together with the Synod Fathers, I express gratitude to those Catholics who are making serious efforts to promote a significant presence in the world of the media, and I ask for an ever wider and more qualified commitment in this regard.[362]

Among the new forms of mass communication, nowadays we need to recognize the increased role of the *internet*, which represents a new forum for making the Gospel heard. Yet we also need to be aware that the virtual world will never be able to replace the real world, and that evangelization will be able to make use of the *virtual world* offered by the new media in order to create meaningful relationships only if it is able to offer the *personal contact* which remains indispensable. In the world of the internet, which enables billions of images to appear on millions of screens throughout the world, *the face of Christ* needs to be seen and his voice heard, for "if there is no room for Christ, there is no room for man".[363]

The Bible and inculturation

114. The mystery of the incarnation tells us that while God always communicates in a con-

---

[361] Cf. *Final Message,* IV, 11; BENEDICT XVI, Message for the 2009 World Day of Social Communications (24 January 2009): *Insegnamenti* V, 1 (2009), 123-127.

[362] Cf. *Propositio* 44.

[363] JOHN PAUL II, Message for the XXXVI World Communications Day (24 January 2002): *Insegnamenti* XXV, 1 (2002), 94-95.

crete history, taking up the cultural codes embedded therein, the same word can and must also be passed on in different cultures, transforming them from within through what Pope Paul VI called *the evangelization of cultures*.[364] The word of God, like the Christian faith itself, has a profoundly *intercultural* character; it is capable of encountering different cultures and in turn enabling them to encounter one another.[365]

Here too we come to appreciate the importance of the *inculturation* of the Gospel.[366] The Church is firmly convinced that the word of God is inherently capable of speaking to all human persons in the context of their own culture: "this conviction springs from the Bible itself, which, right from the Book of Genesis, adopts a universalist stance (cf. *Gen* 1:27-28), maintains it subsequently in the blessing promised to all peoples through Abraham and his offspring (cf. *Gen* 12:3; 18:18), and confirms it definitively in extending to 'all nations' the proclamation of the Gospel".[367] For this reason, inculturation is not to be confused with processes of superficial adapta-

---

[364] Cf. Apostolic Exhortation *Evangelii Nuntiandi* (8 December 1975), 20: AAS 68 (1976), 18-19.

[365] Cf. BENEDICT XVI, Post-Synodal Apostolic Exhortation *Sacramentum Caritatis* (22 February 2007), 78: AAS 99 (2007), 165.

[366] Cf. *Propositio* 48.

[367] PONTIFICAL BIBLICAL COMMISSION, *The Interpretation of the Bible in the Church* (15 April 1993), IV, B: *Enchiridion Vaticanum*, 13, No. 3112.

tion, much less with a confused syncretism which would dilute the uniqueness of the Gospel in an attempt to make it more easily accepted.[368] The authentic paradigm of inculturation is the incarnation itself of the Word: "'Acculturation' or 'inculturation' will truly be a reflection of the incarnation of the Word when a culture, transformed and regenerated by the Gospel, brings forth from its own living tradition original expressions of Christian life, celebration and thought",[369] serving as a leaven within the local culture, enhancing the *semina Verbi* and all those positive elements present within that culture, thus opening it to the values of the Gospel.[370]

Translating the Bible and making it more widely available

115.   The inculturation of God's word is an integral part of the Church's mission in the world, and a decisive moment in this process is the diffusion of the Bible through the precious work of translation into different languages. Here it should always be remembered that the work of translation of the Scriptures had been undertaken "already in the Old Testament period, when the Hebrew text of the Bible was translated oral-

[368] Cf. SECOND VATICAN ECUMENICAL COUNCIL, Decree on the Church's Missionary Activity *Ad Gentes*, 22; PONTIFICAL BIBLICAL COMMISSION, *The Interpretation of the Bible in the Church* (15 April 1993), IV, B: *Enchiridion Vaticanum*, 13, Nos. 3111-3117.

[369] JOHN PAUL II, *Address to the Bishops of Kenya* (7 May 1980), 6: AAS 72 (1980), 497.

[370] Cf. *Instrumentum Laboris*, 56.

ly into Aramaic (*Neh* 8:8,12) and later in written form into Greek. A translation, of course, is always more than a simple transcription of the original texts. The passage from one language to another necessarily involves a change of cultural context: concepts are not identical and symbols have a different meaning, for they come up against other traditions of thought and other ways of life".[371]

During the Synod, it was clear that a number of local Churches still lack a complete translation of the Bible in their own languages. How many people today hunger and thirst for the word of God, yet remain deprived of the "widely available access to Sacred Scripture"[372] desired by the Second Vatican Council! For this reason the Synod considered it important, above all, to train specialists committed to translating the Bible into the various languages.[373] I would encourage the investment of resources in this area. In particular I wish to recommend supporting the work of the Catholic Biblical Federation, with the aim of further increasing the number of translations of sacred Scripture and their wide diffusion.[374] Given the very nature of such an enterprise, it should be carried out as much as

---

[371] PONTIFICAL BIBLICAL COMMISSION, *The Interpretation of the Bible in the Church* (15 April 1993), IV, B: *Enchiridion Vaticanum* 13, No. 3113.

[372] SECOND VATICAN ECUMENICAL COUNCIL, Dogmatic Constitution on Divine Revelation *Dei Verbum*, 22.

[373] Cf. *Propositio* 42.

[374] Cf. *Propositio* 43.

possible in cooperation with the different Bible Societies.

God's word transcends cultural limits

116.   The synodal assembly, in its discussion of the relationship between God's word and cultures, felt the need to reaffirm something that the earliest Christians had experienced beginning on the day of Pentecost (*Acts* 2:1-2). The word of God is capable of entering into and finding expression in various cultures and languages, yet that same word overcomes the limits of individual cultures to create fellowship between different peoples. The Lord's word summons us to advance towards an ever more vast communion. "We escape the limitations of our experience and we enter into the reality that is truly universal. Entering into communion with the word of God, we enter into the communion of the Church which lives the word of God. ... It means going beyond the limits of the individual cultures into the universality that connects all, unites all, makes us all brothers and sisters".[375] The proclamation of God's work thus always demands, of us in the first place, a new exodus, as we leave behind our own limited standards and imaginations in order to make room for the presence of Christ.

[375] BENEDICT XVI, *Homily during the Celebration of Terce at the beginning of the First General Congregation of the Synod of Bishops* (6 October 2008): AAS 100 (2008), 760.

The value of interreligious dialogue

117.   The Church considers an essential part of
the proclamation of the word to consist in encounter, dialogue and cooperation with all people of good will, particularly with the followers
of the different religious traditions of humanity.
This is to take place without forms of syncretism
and relativism, but along the lines indicated by
the Second Vatican Council's Declaration *Nostra
Aetate* and subsequently developed by the magisterium of the Popes.[376] Nowadays the quickened
pace of globalization makes it possible for people
of different cultures and religions to be in closer
contact. This represents a providential opportunity for demonstrating how authentic religiosity can
foster relationships of universal fraternity. Today,
in our frequently secularized societies, it is very
important that the religions be capable of fostering a mentality that sees Almighty God as the

[376] Among numerous interventions of various genres,
see: JOHN PAUL II, Encyclical Letter *Dominum et Vivificantem* (18
May 1986): AAS 78 (1986), 809-900; Encyclical Letter *Redemptoris Missio* (7 December 1990): AAS 83 (1991), 249-340; Addresses and Homilies in Assisi for the 27 October 1986 Day
of Prayer for Peace: *Insegnamenti* IX, 2 (1986), 1249-1273; Day
of Prayer for World Peace (24 January 2002): *Insegnamenti* XXV,
1 (2002), 97-108; CONGREGATION FOR THE DOCTRINE OF THE
FAITH, Declaration *Dominus Iesus* on the Unicity and Salvific
Universality of Jesus Christ and of the Church (6 August 2000):
AAS 92 (2000), 742-765.

foundation of all good, the inexhaustible source of the moral life, and the bulwark of a profound sense of universal brotherhood.

In the Judeo-Christian tradition, for example, one finds a moving witness to God's love for all peoples: in the covenant with Noah he joins them in one great embrace symbolized by the "bow in the clouds" (*Gen* 9:13,14,16) and, according to the words of the prophets, he desires to gather them into a single universal family (cf. *Is* 2:2ff; 42:6; 66:18-21; *Jer* 4:2; *Ps* 47). Evidence of a close connection between a relationship with God and the ethics of love for everyone is found in many great religious traditions.

Dialogue between Christians and Muslims

118.   Among the various religions the Church also looks with respect to Muslims, who adore the one God.[377] They look to Abraham and worship God above all through prayer, almsgiving and fasting. We acknowledge that the Islamic tradition includes countless biblical figures, symbols and themes. Taking up the efforts begun by the Venerable John Paul II, I express my hope that the trust-filled relationships established between Christians and Muslims over the years will continue to develop in a spirit of sincere and respectful

[377] Cf. SECOND VATICAN ECUMENICAL COUNCIL, Declaration on the Relation of the Church to Non-Christian Religions *Nostra Aetate*, 3.

dialogue.[378] In this dialogue the Synod asked for a deeper reflection on respect for life as a fundamental value, the inalienable rights of men and women, and their equal dignity. Taking into account the important distinction to be made between the socio-political order and the religious order, the various religions must make their specific contribution to the common good. The Synod asked Conferences of Bishops, wherever it is appropriate and helpful, to encourage meetings aimed at helping Christians and Muslims to come to better knowledge of one another, in order to promote the values which society needs for a peaceful and positive coexistence.[379]

Dialogue with other religions

119.   Here too I wish to voice the Church's respect for the ancient religions and spiritual traditions of the various continents. These contain values which can greatly advance understanding between individuals and peoples.[380] Frequently we note a consonance with values expressed also in their religious books, such as, in Buddhism, respect for life, contemplation, silence, simplicity; in Hinduism, the sense of the sacred, sacrifice and fasting; and again, in Confucianism, family and

[378] Cf. BENEDICT XVI, *Address to Ambassadors of Predominantly Muslim Countries Accredited to the Holy See* (25 September 2006): AAS 98 (2006), 704-706.
[379] Cf. *Propositio* 53.
[380] Cf. *Propositio* 50.

social values. We are also gratified to find in other religious experiences a genuine concern for the transcendence of God, acknowledged as Creator, as well as respect for life, marriage and the family, and a strong sense of solidarity.

Dialogue and religious freedom

120. All the same, dialogue would not prove fruitful unless it included authentic respect for each person and the ability of all freely to practise their religion. Hence the Synod, while encouraging cooperation between the followers of the different religions, also pointed out "the need for the freedom to profess one's religion, privately and publicly, and freedom of conscience to be effectively guaranteed to all believers":[381] indeed, "respect and dialogue require reciprocity in all spheres, especially in that which concerns basic freedoms, more particularly religious freedom. Such respect and dialogue foster peace and understanding between peoples".[382]

[381] *Ibid.*.

[382] JOHN PAUL II, *Address at the Meeting with Young Muslims in Casablanca, Morocco* (19 August 1985), 5: AAS 78 (1986), 99.

CONCLUSION

God's definitive word

121.   At the conclusion of these reflections with which I have sought to gather up and examine more fully the rich fruits of the Twelfth Ordinary General Assembly of the Synod of Bishops on the word of God in the life and mission of the Church, I wish once more to encourage all the People of God, pastors, consecrated persons and the laity, to become increasingly familiar with the sacred Scriptures. We must never forget that all authentic and living Christian spirituality is based on *the word of God proclaimed, accepted, celebrated and meditated upon in the Church.* This deepening relationship with the divine word will take place with even greater enthusiasm if we are conscious that, in Scripture and the Church's living Tradition, we stand before God's definitive word on the cosmos and on history.

The Prologue of John's Gospel leads us to ponder the fact that everything that exists is under the sign of the Word. The Word goes forth from the Father, comes to dwell in our midst and then returns to the Father in order to bring with him the whole of creation which was made in him and for him. The Church now carries out her mission in eager expectation of the eschatological manifestation of the Bridegroom: "the Spirit and the bride say: 'Come!'" (*Rev* 22:17). This expectation is never passive; rather it is a missionary drive to proclaim the word of God which heals and redeems every man. Today too the Risen Jesus says to us: "Go into all the world and proclaim the Gospel to the whole creation" (*Mk* 16:15).

New evangelization and a new hearing

122.   Our own time, then, must be increasingly marked by a new hearing of God's word and a new evangelization. Recovering the centrality of the divine word in the Christian life leads us to appreciate anew the deepest meaning of the forceful appeal of Pope John Paul II: to pursue the *missio ad gentes* and vigorously to embark upon the new evangelization, expecially in those nations where the Gospel has been forgotten or meets with indifference as a result of widespread secularism. May the Holy Spirit awaken a hunger and thirst for the word of God, and raise up zealous heralds and witnesses of the Gospel.

Following the example of the great Apostle of the Nations, who changed the course of his life after hearing the voice of the Lord (cf. *Acts* 9:1-30), let us too hear God's word as it speaks to us, ever personally, here and now. The Holy Spirit, we are told in the *Acts of the Apostles*, set Paul and

Barnabas apart to proclaim and spread the Good News (cf. 13:2). In our day too, the Holy Spirit constantly calls convinced and persuasive hearers and preachers of the word of the Lord.

The word and joy

123.   The greater our openness to God's word, the more will we be able to recognize that today too the mystery of Pentecost is taking place in God's Church. The Spirit of the Lord continues to pour out his gifts upon the Church to guide us into all truth, to show us the meaning of the Scriptures and to make us credible heralds of the word of salvation before the world. Thus we return to the First Letter of Saint John. In God's word, we too have heard, we too have seen and touched the Word of life. We have welcomed by grace the proclamation that eternal life has been revealed, and thus we have come to acknowledge our fellowship with one another, with those who have gone before us marked with the sign of faith, and with all those who throughout the world hear the word, celebrate the Eucharist and by their lives bear witness to charity. This proclamation has been shared with us – the Apostle John reminds us – so that "our joy may be complete" (*1 Jn* 1:4).

The synodal assembly enabled us to experience all that Saint John speaks of: the proclamation of the word creates *communion* and brings about *joy*. This is a profound joy which has its origin in the very heart of the trinitarian life and which is communicated to us in the Son. This joy is an ineffable gift which the world cannot give. Celebrations can be organized, but not joy. According to the Scripture, joy is the fruit of the Holy Spirit (cf. *Gal* 5:22) who enables us to enter into the word and enables the divine word to enter into us and to bear fruit for eternal life. By proclaiming God's word in the power of the Holy Spirit, we also wish to share the source of true joy, not a superficial and fleeting joy, but the joy born of the awareness that the Lord Jesus alone has words of everlasting life (cf. *Jn* 6:68).

"Mater Verbi et Mater laetitiae"

124. This close relationship between God's word and joy is evident in the Mother of God. Let us recall the words of Saint Elizabeth: "Blessed is she who believed that there would be a fulfilment of what was spoken to her by the Lord" (*Lk* 1:45). Mary is blessed because she has faith, because she believed, and in this faith she received the Word of God into her womb in order to give him to the world. The joy born of the Word can now expand to all those who, by faith, let themselves be changed by God's word. The *Gospel of Luke* presents this mystery of hearing and joy in two texts. Jesus says: "My mother and my brothers are those who hear the word of God and do it" (8:21). And in reply to a woman from the crowd who blesses the womb that bore him

and the breasts that nursed him, Jesus reveals the secret of true joy: "Blessed rather are those who hear the word of God and obey it!" (11:28). Jesus points out Mary's true grandeur, making it possible for each of us to attain that blessedness which is born of the word received and put into practice. I remind all Christians that our personal and communal relationship with God depends on our growing familiarity with the word of God. Finally, I turn to every man and woman, including those who have fallen away from the Church, who have left the faith or who have never heard the proclamation of salvation. To everyone the Lord says: "Behold, I stand at the door and knock; if anyone hears my voice and opens the door, I will come in to him and eat with him, and he with me" (*Rev* 3:20).

May every day of our lives thus be shaped by a renewed encounter with Christ, the Word of the Father made flesh: he stands at the beginning and the end, and "in him all things hold together" (*Col* 1:17). Let us be silent in order to hear the Lord's word and to meditate upon it, so that by the working of the Holy Spirit it may remain in our hearts and speak to us all the days of our lives. In this way the Church will always be renewed and rejuvenated, thanks to the word of the Lord which remains for ever (cf. *1 Pet* 1:25; *Is* 40:8). Thus we too will enter into the great nuptial dialogue which concludes sacred Scripture: "The Spirit and the bride say: 'Come'. And let everyone who hears say: 'Come!'" The one who testifies to these things, says: 'Surely I am coming soon!'. Amen. Come, Lord Jesus!'". (*Rev* 22:17, 20).

Given in Rome, at Saint Peter's, on 30 September, the Memorial of Saint Jerome, in the year 2010, the sixth of my Pontificate.

Benedictus PP XVI

INDEX

PART THREE

VERBUM MUNDO

the WORD among us®
The Spirit of Catholic Living

This book was published by The Word Among Us. For nearly thirty years, The Word Among Us has been answering the call of the Second Vatican Council to help Catholic laypeople encounter Christ in the Scriptures—a call reiterated recently by Pope Benedict XVI and a Synod of Bishops.

The name of our company comes from the prologue to the Gospel of John and reflects the vision and purpose of all of our publications: to be an instrument of the Spirit, whose desire is to manifest Jesus' presence in and to the children of God. In this way, we hope to contribute to the church's ongoing mission of proclaiming the gospel to the world and growing ever more deeply in our love for the Lord.

Our monthly devotional magazine, *The Word Among Us*, features meditations on the daily and Sunday Mass readings, and currently reaches more than one million Catholics in North America each year and another 500,000 Catholics in 100 countries. Our press division has published nearly 180 books and Bible studies over the past ten years.

To learn more about who we are and what we publish, log on to our Web site at **www.wau.org**. There you will find a variety of Catholic resources that will help you grow in your faith.

Embrace His Word, Listen to God . . .